To Rabbi R
from

February, 1994

Via Cracow and Beirut

A Survivor's Saga

Richard Stern

VIA CRACOW AND BEIRUT   A SURVIVOR'S SAGA

Copyright © Richard Stern 1994

All Rights Reserved

No part of this book may be reproduced in any form,
by photocopying or by any electronic or mechanical means,
including information storage or retrieval systems,
without permission in writing from both the copyright owner
and the publisher of this book.

ISBN 1 85863 111 4

First Published 1994 by
MINERVA PRESS
2, Old Brompton Road,
London SW7 3DQ.

Printed in Great Britain by
B.W.D. Ltd., Northolt, Middlesex

Via Cracow and Beirut

A Survivor's Saga

About the Author

Gabriel Richard Stern, known generally as Richard Stern, was born and educated in Poland. The outbreak of the war interrupted his studies of Chemistry at Cracow University. He escaped from the German occupation eastwards but was arrested by Soviet Police and imprisoned. After fourteen months in various prisons he was sentenced without trial to three years Forced Labour Camp. He served eight months in the far North when, thanks to an amnesty, he was freed to join the Polish Army which was being formed in the Soviet Union. He fought at Monte Cassino, was wounded, awarded the Cross of Valour and promoted to the rank of officer.

After the war he continued his studies of Chemistry at the American University of Beirut and later Chemical Engineering in London.

Married with three children, he lives now in Bournemouth. Over many years had been engaged in helping Soviet Jewry and chairing the local branch of the British Technion Society.

ACKNOWLEDGEMENTS

I acknowledge with gratitude the wise comments from Sidney Silverman regarding the structure of the book and am particularly grateful to him for suggesting the title.

Special thanks go to my dear wife, Esther, without whose encouragement and gentle pressure these Memoirs would not have been written.

CONTENTS

	Page
Preface	vii
My Town Jedrzejow	9
Attack on Poland	16
Soviet Troops Enter Poland	19
Hunger Strike	31
The Second Hunger Strike	34
Interrogation	38
Communication with My Brother, Henry	44
Voroshilovgrad	46
The Small Cell in Voroshilovgrad Prison	48
Transit Camps (Etap)	52
Starobielsk	57
The Sentence	65
Journey to Forced Labour Camp (Corrective Camp)	67
Zhith Boodesh	69
The Forced Labour Camp, Chibiu (Kotlas)	71
The 'Surgery'	81
The Camp Aristocracy	83
My 'Friend' Ilya	86
The Camp Office	91
The Tool Shed	97
Watchman	101
Nazi Germany Attacks the Soviet Union	105
Supervisor of 'Bezprisornikh' (juvenile delinquents)	107
The Amnesty	110
Guzar	115
Exodus from the Soviet Union	121
Tobruk and El-Alamein	125
Transport to Palestine	128
North Africa and the Soviet Union	131
We Continue Our Journey to Palestine	133
Leave in Palestine	141

Italy - Our Final Destination	148
The Battle for the Monastery	163
My Friend Jurek	168
Allied Forces in Rome	172
'Holidays' in Egypt	173
My Holiday in Rome	175
Victory in Europe (VE-Day)	178
An Hour of Remembrance	180
A New Perspective	182
Lebanon	185
Transport to Britain	195
Jurek in London	196
Epilogue	206
Maps	211
References	213

Preface

These Memoirs, though written many years after the events they describe, have nevertheless the quality of complete authenticity, because they are mostly based on notes taken only a few years after the war ended.

Besides, it can be safely stated that the experience of invasion of Poland by the Germans and their rule of the occupied territories cannot be easily forgotten.

The Pact between the Soviet Union and Nazi Germany in 1939 delivered a tremendous blow to the morale of Polish people, and dashed the hopes of those Jews who sought a safe haven behind the newly established border between yesterday's antagonists and the now great 'friends'.

Life in Soviet prisons and Forced Labour Camps was marked by continuous hunger and hard work in the latter and no doubt left indelible memories, but it must be stressed that there was no organised terror, no planned annihilation or planned genocide as in Nazi German death camps.

Survival under dangerously critical conditions is a result of resilience and luck, and in my case, the latter was in greater proportion than the former.

MY TOWN JEDRZEJOW (pron. Yendgeuv)

My little town in Southern Poland, Jedrzejow, where I was born and brought up and whose foundation goes back to the Middle Ages, had a famous 12th century Monastery, a parish church, a market place, cobble stone streets, a small number of two storey houses and a population of about 12,000 of whom a third were Jews. The area round the town was agricultural with a large proportion of forests. Close to where we lived there were meadows through which meandered a little stream called Brzeznica, carrying its water into the river Nida, a tributary of the largest Polish river, the Vistula.

The little river was my playground when I was a child. Together with my friend Haskel, a year my senior, whose mother, a widow, scraped a living as a washerwoman, we used to spend many hours in bright summer sunshine at the stream, paddling, catching minnows and floating little boats made of empty matchboxes. The meadow was a pasture used by a few very poor people who owned one or two cows as the only source of income.

A corner of the green field served as a football 'ground' where my first football playing experience using a rag ball was gained. Later, probably at the age of seven, I became a member of a football team, whose captain was Haskel and the ball we played with was no longer made of rags: it was a genuine cow's or perhaps pig's bladder, which one could buy from a butcher shop for a few groshen (pennies).

The situation changed completely when at the age of 11 the Hebrew school 'Yabneh' which I went to from the age of 6 wound up and I was put into the nearest State Primary School, which was situated close to the Monastery. This physical closeness to the centre of local Catholicism had a great influence on the atmosphere prevailing at the school. The change-over was quite dramatic. My school mates were no longer exclusively Jewish; in fact I was now the only Jewish boy in the form.

It took me quite a while to get used to the new environment. At my previous school we had to keep our school caps on all the time and here the minute you entered the classroom you had to bare your head, because there was a crucifix on the wall. It was an offence not to do so. However, after about a fortnight I struck up a friendship with a class mate who lived in our neighbourhood, and since he came from a poor and uneducated family, he was pleased to associate with me. Thanks to him I began to feel more at ease and gradually adapted myself to the new conditions.

The social structure of the population in my town was quite well defined. The top of the social ladder was occupied by the few doctors, lawyers and dentists, who were always addressed as "doctor". Then came the teachers of the two secondary schools who were generally addressed "professor", then much lower down the social scale came owners of the few factories, richer shop keepers, and lower still, small shop keepers, and at the very bottom: artisans, craftsmen and manual workers of various kinds. Land owners were a class of their own. They lived on their estates, behaved like feudal lords and were addressed "your lordship".

The Jewish community was represented in all the social layers except in the group of teachers. There were two Jewish doctors, two lawyers, four families - owners of a brewery, two flour mills and a small nail and shoe-heel protector factory, but the vast majority of Jews were shop keepers, tailors, carpenters and of no fixed occupation. The Civil Service, the Law Courts, schools and local administration did not employ Jews and though there was no official anti-Jewish law, no Jew had ever been successful in obtaining employment in those institutions.

Large numbers of Jews lived in poverty and were recipients of help from the Community Office to which the richer members contributed. There were in town a number of primary State schools, where education was free, one Grammar school (called Gymnazium), privately maintained, and one State Teachers Training College which did not accept Jews. There was also a private Hebrew primary school 'Yabneh' as mentioned above, where I received my early Jewish education.

There was, of course, a Beit Midrash, housing a synagogue and a Talmud Torah (a minor Yeshivah) and a number of shtiblech (private accommodation) where services were held on

Friday night and Saturday morning. The majority of the Jewish population was strictly orthodox and on Shabbat one could hardly buy anything in the centre of town because all Jewish shops were closed. The vast majority of Jews, particularly the older generation, spoke and wrote Yiddish, but younger people, having been to Polish schools, spoke among themselves Polish and with their parents, Yiddish.

There were several Jewish organisations, Zionist and non-Zionist, religious and non-religious. 'Hashomer Hatzair' gathered left wing oriented Youth, whereas Yabneh and Akiba - the more traditional and observant. There was also a small group of Bund supporters, who were anti-Zionists and proclaimed solidarity with the non-Jewish Socialist Workers Party. With the rise of nationalism and anti-Semitism in the thirties in Poland, Zionist organisations grew in strength.

In pre-war Poland Yiddish was not only a means of oral communication; it flourished as the printed word in the form of several daily newspapers, weekly magazines, books and a variety of other publications. The political and social conditions of Jews in Poland started to deteriorate several years before the war, but in spite of difficulties, Jewish culture asserted itself healthily.

The three years I spent at the Primary School were probably the happiest of my early teenage period. I was reasonably sociable, made friends easily, particularly with girls in the form, did well at learning, and played games tolerably well.

There was however, one difficulty: I did not attend school on Saturdays and had to rely on the good will of some of my non-Jewish colleagues whom I visited on the following Sunday to inform me what happened at school so that I could do my homework for Monday. This ritual carried on right through my secondary education until matriculation, for it would have been completely out of the question for me to attend school on Shabbat.

The children who attended my school came mostly from poor homes, though there was a reasonable minority of those whose upbringing showed a middle class influence. The form master's task was to inculcate good manners, courtesy, pride in good appearance; in a word, to civilise us. This went often too far and became at times ridiculous. We were supposed to open the door for a lady, to get up when a woman entered the room, to kiss the hand when shaking hands with a woman, to offer to carry whatever she might carry at the time, including her handbag, etc., etc. You were supposed to be chivalrous and often a saying was, half seriously, quoted: 'you mustn't hit a woman not even with a flower'. Doffing one's hat was an obligatory form of greeting when passing friends and acquaintances in the street and tracing a large ellipse in the air when taking off your hat was considered a mark of exceptional respect.

Hygiene was given a lot of attention and one particular form master ordered us every morning to put our hands on the bench for inspection of our nails. That was the time when the first romantic love affairs sprouted and communication with the girl sitting a few feet away was effected by the use of a simplified Morse code.

At the age of 14 I took an entry examination to the Grammar School (Gymnazium) and with the help of my elder brothers, who by now were the main providers for our family of seven, I started my secondary education. Here I was reunited with a few of my Jewish colleagues from the early years of the Hebrew School. Apart from imbibing Polish culture and enjoying poetry by Mickiewicz and Slowacki and books by Sienkiewicz, I started to be interested in politics and soon became a radical. The early thirties was a time of strong polarisation of political views: Fascism and Nazism were in the ascendancy and gathered support from the upper and middle classes of society and this growing movement was valiantly opposed by the declining numbers of socialists and communists.

My sympathies lay with the latter group though I could not reconcile myself with the idea of 'dictatorship' of the proletariat. I abhorred the idea of dictatorship. Zionism was to me then too selfish a concept and I dreamed of higher aims: of reconciliation of social conflicts, of co-operation and harmony among nations, of a classless society and all the qualities of a truly free and liberal mode of living. These ideals underwent with time some changes under pressure of reality, lost a lot of their romanticism, but remained in essence with me for the years up to matriculation and the three years of my studies of Chemistry at the Cracow University.

When I returned home at the end of June 1939 from University people's minds were already occupied with the fateful thought of the possibility of war; however, the talks between Britain, France and the Soviet Union about a friendship and co-operation pact raised hopes of an establishment of a strong military front against the appetites of the Third Reich. These hopes were shattered when towards the end of August the talks broke down, the consequence of which was a free hand for Hitler to fulfil his intended 'Drang nach Osten.'

ATTACK ON POLAND

At dawn on Friday, the 1st of September, Warsaw, Lodz, Cracow and several other cities, all of them open and undefended, were bombed. This was followed by the quick invasion of the Western part of Poland. Jews had no illusions as to the future under Nazi rule, but no one could have foreseen the enormity of the catastrophe to come.

When we heard on the radio that Britain had declared war on Germany, our hearts leaped for joy and there was generally a deep and unshaken belief that the Nazis would soon learn their lesson, that the might of the British Empire would stop the Teutonic hordes, and that it was only a matter of a short time to the glorious moment of the invaders' complete defeat. Instead the tragic reality unfolded relentlessly.

The German Forces rolled on with lightening speed and two days after the first bomb fell, thousands of refugees from the Western part of Poland were making their way eastwards, causing chaos on the roads and filling our little town to capacity. These were followed by German armoured units pushing forward, to the remaining, still unoccupied, parts of the country. People were frightened to go out into the street; shops were closed, normal life ceased.

Rumours began to go round that some Jewish shops had been broken into by Polish peasants led and encouraged by Volksdeutschen, that is, people of German origin who had lived in Poland and carried Polish passports but had suddenly discovered their faith and declared their loyalty to the German Reich. Soon these rumours were proved true many times over.

Jews were robbed by local louts and peasants from neighbouring villages with the encouragement of not only Volksdeutschen but also German military Police, and shops were quickly emptied.

The German Command issued orders forbidding Jews to attend the only cinema in town and Jewish children were banned from schools. Hostages were being taken and some of them were shot in the market place. Jews were rounded up for work on the road but there were no mass arrests and there appeared to be no plan for continuous or increasing oppression. The instinct of survival under any circumstances searched for a chink of light in the prevailing darkness, and since there was a momentary lull in the anti-Jewish orders, there was some hope that a sort of normality under the imposed constraints would eventually emerge.

Thoughts were turned to the question of schooling for Jewish children and I intended, together with Maurice Silberstein, a local teacher of Hebrew, who was at one time my teacher, well known and loved by the community, to organise some classes in a private place. Silberstein would teach Hebrew and Torah and I - secular subjects. Before we could even work out some sort of plan, the project was killed by a decree that any kind of gathering in private or public places was forbidden under the pain of death.

A further order required to take all radio sets (there was no television yet) in one's possession to an appointed office in the Town Hall. Telephone and Post Office services stopped functioning, thus all communication with the outer world ceased.

SOVIET TROOPS ENTER POLAND

After the break-up of the negotiations between the Soviet Union and the Western Powers, Stalin signed a non-aggression pact with Hitler (the infamous Ribbentrop-Molotov Agreement) on the basis of which Germany would annex the Western and Central part of Poland and the Soviet Union the Eastern part. Consequently, the Red Army entered Polish territory on the 17th September, and after overcoming the resistance of the by then greatly enfeebled units of the Polish Army, invaded the Eastern provinces, and a tentative border was established between the two powers.

The initial relative calm quickly came to an end and then followed an imposition of further restrictions on the Jewish community and a rounding up of young Jewish men, ostensibly for work in some army camps, usually some distance from home. This was a signal for many to make their way to Eastern Poland which by now was under Soviet rule. In our innocence we believed that our Eastern neighbour was a haven of peace and freedom and it was natural to try to run away to that country.

I got together with several friends of similar age and we decided to make our way to Lvov. It wasn't easy to reconcile myself with the thought of leaving my parents, a brother and two sisters and run away, but that was also their wish and so, as not to rouse suspicion of the local railway station officials who knew us, we decided to leave the town by horse and cart to the neighbouring town Miechow.

My parents insisted on providing me with some money, but, since it was unwise in the prevailing circumstances to carry substantial sums, my brother, who was a dental technician, gave me two gold platelets, about one cm diameter and one mm thick, the sort of material used to make tooth caps. These were easy to hide and could, when needed, provide enough for a few weeks living.

In Miechow lived my sister who was the eldest in my family of eight children. She was married with two young daughters. She realised the seriousness of the situation, and though reticent on the subject, it was obvious that she viewed the future with foreboding. She was glad, however, that I was trying to escape to freedom. When I told her about the two little gold discs, she advised me to hide them in the seam of my coat, which, I thought, was a good idea, and so she opened one of the seams under the coat lining, stuck the discs in and stitched up the seam and the lining.

Later in the evening I met with my group and we took the train to Cracow. The hour's journey to Cracow passed without incident. We intended to take the train to Sanok, a small town on the river San which became the border between the now 'friendly' countries. While waiting on the platform for the train - it was early evening - an SS officer approached us and asked: 'Jude?' This was the first direct encounter with Nazism in

came in holding a note book, which turned out to be a diary which he found in the luggage. He opened it and began to read a poem in German. It was 'Der Fischer', a popular piece of poetry by Goethe. The SS man stopped in the middle and shrieked in an uncontrollable rage: 'you Jewish swine - how dare you meddle in our German literature!'. This followed by a further round of blows.

The orgy of shouting and beating went on till dawn when they ordered us to line up at the exit door, each one to say 'danke fur die Arbeit' and leave. Our belongings were scattered all over the hall. Most of the best clothes, watches, fountain pens etc. were missing. We collected what remained and hurriedly left the hateful building. By then the group had dispersed and only three of us: my friend and his girl friend, who waited outside trembling and in tears, and myself.

We walked along at a fast pace to the town centre, dazed and in fear. Suddenly a German army lorry with two soldiers in the driving seat stopped and the driver asked us in a friendly voice where we wished to go. 'To Sanok' we answered hesitatingly. 'Climb in - I am going there'. We didn't know whether to trust him but the desire to get away from that hateful place was too strong to resist the offer. It looked and sounded so very providential. The journey lasted about three hours. We could not help wondering whether the drive would end uneventfully or disastrously, and we wished to see the end of it as quickly as possible. We arrived in Sanok in the early hours of the morning. The driver stopped in the market place and informed us that it was our destination. Still somewhat suspicious we alighted from the lorry and thanked him for his kindness.

We stood in the market place wondering what to do next, when a man approached us, introduced himself and asked whether we needed any help. He was Jewish and he guessed our intentions. He took us home and introduced us to his wife and two children, gave us a meal and after we had told them what happened to us, they insisted that we should have some sleep. They offered us their own beds. A most remarkable, almost biblical degree of hospitality. It brought to my mind the story of the strangers who appeared in front of Abraham's tent and of Abraham washing their feet and ordering a feast for them.

We needed a guide to smuggle us over the border which ran along the river San. Our host promised to help and indeed he put us in touch with a Polish farmer whose house was near the river, and who was prepared, for an agreed price, to take us across the river into, what we thought to be, the promised land.

That night we were taken to the farmhouse, where there were already about a dozen young Jewish people - all gathered for the same purpose. We were resting, sitting and lying wherever one could, most on the floor, waiting for a signal to go. It came soon after midnight. Silently we followed our guide, one behind the others walking over soggy fields and heath land to the river bank. The sky was moonless and the river dark, the current, luckily, sufficiently fast and noisy to drown the sound of our movement. We were, naturally, very anxious. The thought of possible betrayal, or excessive river depth or any other mishap, played on one's mind.

Fortunately, the water was only two to three feet deep. The crossing took probably no more than twenty minutes but it seemed interminable. When we reached the other river bank I wanted to shout for joy but the feeling had to be suppressed. We were now free from the Germans, but had to avoid Soviet patrols, who, we were told, would open fire on anyone crossing the border, or would send refugees back to the Germans. Our guide led us to a small house standing about half a mile away from the river, belonging to his friend, a partner in the smuggling business.

Dawn was breaking. We were now to travel by horse and wagon to the nearest little town. The group divided into two, eight and seven, and I and my two friends were to make the journey first. By now, in fine spirit, we were trundling along an unmade country road to freedom. For some hours the road was completely empty, not a soul to be seen.

Suddenly two militiamen with rifles slung over their shoulders appeared from a nearby wood. They approached us, stopped the driver and asked where he was going and who were the people he was taking. There ensued a short conversation in Ukrainian which I could not understand, and an order was given to the driver to follow the militiamen. It was obvious that we had been arrested and were being taken to the Police Station.

We were led into the Police Station where, after the usual questioning about identity and purpose of our journey, we were told that as soon as the veracity of our statements was confirmed, we would be allowed to go. In the meantime we would be detained. We were ordered to follow a militiaman while another kept an eye on us from the back of the group. It was soon obvious where they were taking us. The building with the small barred and mostly blocked windows was unmistakably the local prison, and that was the place we were approaching. My brother, Henry, was in Lvov (Lemberg) and I knew his address. I decided to contact him but I realised that it would be impossible to do it the normal way by postal service, and our 'chaperons' became increasingly unfriendly. On the way from the Police Station to the prison I managed to scribble a few words on a card, addressed it and dropped it inconspicuously in the hope that somebody would pick it up and send it to my brother.

On reaching the gate of the prison the relative civility of our guards ended. Prison guards with rifles and bayonets on the ready were keeping order. We were led to a big room, ordered to strip completely while our belongings were thoroughly searched. Some of the group still had some money, watches, penknives, safety razors, fountain pens, pencils - all these objects were taken away and recorded. Then followed the requisition of belts, braces and shoelaces and a thorough body search. They looked into one's mouth, under arms, ordered to crouch down and inspected the rectum and soles. After the search we were given back only our clothes, all other objects were withheld. We were then led away and shut in cells.

In that small prison they kept us only three days after which we were taken by lorry under strict guard to a much larger prison in Sambor, which, though in Poland until a short time before, had by then been administered totally by Ukrainian personnel. My cell, designed to hold 6 people, now held 18, of whom there were 5 Jews, 3 Ukrainians and the rest Poles. The cell had two small windows with iron bars, three quarters of each window being covered on the outside with wooden boards, so that only a narrow strip of sky could be seen. There were wooden bunks covered with straw mattresses (palliasses), but there were no blankets or pillows.

There were no toilet facilities, only a bucket in the corner of the cell. The shock of being treated like a criminal was too great to bear. It was difficult to understand why we deserved to be shut up in prison. There must have been some mistake, we thought, some procedural hitch. It couldn't be true that they ignored the fact that we had run away from the Nazis and came here as friends, who wished to be loyal to the Government and serve the country. In my innocence I believed that the whole business was a temporary aberration which would, no doubt, be corrected shortly.

With these thoughts we tried to comfort ourselves and were looking forward with confidence to a brighter future. But three weeks went by with no change in our situation. We decided to do something about it. We demanded to see the Prosecutor (Procuror) or the prison Governor. The following morning the Governor came and asked what was our problem. He appeared to be civil and was prepared to listen to our complaints, but when one of us addressed him by 'Tovarish Nachalnik' (Comrade Commandant), he promptly retorted: 'I am not your comrade'! It was still natural for us to show friendship to the new country, and addressing the Governor as Comrade was a spontaneous manifestation of that feeling. His reply came like a stab in the heart.

We asked him to arrange for our case to be considered promptly and to kindly reduce the awful overcrowding in the cell. The Governor listened carefully and promised to meet our requests. As a result of that visit, frustration and anger had been temporarily relieved by hopeful expectation. In the meantime we settled down to the prison routine.

The clatter of dishes and the noise along the corridor of the wheeled cauldron with black surrogate chicory coffee were a welcome signal to line up at the door for breakfast. This was also the time when one received the bread ration for the whole day. With the bread came a portion of the black coffee. The bread, about one pound of it, was to become the sustaining power, the thin border between subsistence and starvation. Speculation as to our destiny was rife. The occasional glance through the open door while the coffee was being dished out might provide some clue, a sound through the wall, an unguarded word from a prison warder - these were sufficient to spin a web of possibilities and even certainties.

We were promised an interview with the Procuror as soon as administration formalities were concluded, but several weeks passed by without anyone being taken out from the cell or any of the officials calling. The prison day was a grey routine punctuated by the morning bread and coffee and evening meal, which consisted of groat soup or cabbage soup in which on occasions floated a piece of fish or meat. Hunger started to be felt generally, some suffered acutely. To paraphrase Dr. Johnson, 'hunger concentrates one's mind admirably'. What to do with the bread ration became quite a problem - to eat it up at once in the morning, which was everybody's powerful inclination, or to divide it and have some later in the day? It was a challenge which called for extreme willpower and only a few succeeded in keeping a piece of bread till midday.

There was nothing to read and we were not taken out for walks. The only time we left the cell was when we were taken for a few minutes to an open lavatory under the guarding eyes of the prison warder, often a wardress. A bare electric bulb was on all night, and since there wasn't enough room on the bunks some of us slept on the floor, using our trousers for a mattress and jacket or overcoat for a blanket.

The physical closeness of people in the cell did not make it easy to make friends. On the contrary, some resentment surfaced from time to time and you had to control your temper on such occasions.

I got to know more closely three people, Jack Domb and his brother-in-law whose name escapes me, and Simon - a more educated man than the other two. Simon was a business man whose business was exporting pigs, a most unusual occupation for a Jew. I found in Simon a friend with whom I could speak openly without fear of being denounced and he, equally, trusted me. He often confided in me telling me about his family, his only child, his life in Sosnowiec, a small town in Silesia, and his pig business. My friendship with Simon brought me a tangible benefit. I slept next to him on the floor, and since he had a large overcoat, it covered me too. Days dragged on interminably. Some managed to kill time by telling stories, by inventing games, though there was no material of any sort to use in games, others sank into silence and melancholy.

Simon and I tried to get some exercise by walking there and back the length of the cell using the 'prisoner's step', that is, left foot and partner's right foot in step, instead of the usual marching order. This made it easier to turn round when reaching the wall of the cell. The cell was bursting at the seams, but apparently it was not full enough according to the prison authorities, for one morning another two men were brought in. It became unbearable.

The new people were not refugees from German occupied Poland, they were local public servants. They told us that mass arrests were being made among the local population, that prisons were filling up to capacity, and to their knowledge no one had yet been let out. The news was most depressing.

HUNGER STRIKE

Several of us decided to do something about the apparent hopeless situation, and since the only weapon a prisoner has in an extremely well guarded prison is to go on hunger strike, we were ready to start it. We discussed the matter with the rest of the people and achieved complete agreement for action.

The following morning, when the coffee and bread were brought to the door of our cell, there was no queue. The warder looked in and asked why we were not lined up for breakfast and when one of us explained the reason, he shook his head and shut the door. Some time later the senior warder came in and said that refusal to take food was a punishable offence under Soviet law, and if we carried on like that, we would only worsen our chances. Our reply was clear: 'we shall continue our strike unless we are given the opportunity to speak to the prosecutor or to the prison Governor'.

Later that day came the Governor. He delivered a little speech saying that there was no need to demonstrate, that our cases were being considered and within a fortnight we should know the outcome. This was reassuring and we decided to call off the hunger strike. There was a heightened feeling of success, and we settled down to the daily prison life.

Among us were two young Ukrainians, Vasil and Nicolai. Vasil was the son of a Greek-Orthodox priest. Both these men were caught on the Russian/German border when they tried to cross over to the Germans whom they considered their friends. Before the war the south-eastern part of Poland had a large number of Ukrainians, most of whom were strongly nationalistic and hostile to Poland. Any Ukrainian national activities used to be rigorously suppressed by the Polish authorities by what was called euphemistically, 'pacification' actions, and as a revenge for one such action, the Polish Minister of Home Affairs, Stanislav Pieracki, was assassinated by Ukrainian activists.

Somebody in the cell whispered that these two young men were directly involved in the assassination. They hated Russians but perhaps more so, the Poles; their sympathy lay with the Germans, but, of course, they would not openly profess their convictions.

Vasil had a black beard, sparkling black eyes and an engaging smile. His friend, Nicolai, tall, blue-eyed with a flowing ginger beard, was quiet and closed-in, an introvert. At first they kept to themselves, spoke Ukrainian and sang Ukrainian songs in perfect harmony. After some weeks, when I got to know them better, Vasil suggested to me to teach me Ukrainian. He showed me a bit of pencil which he managed to hide between the planks of the bunk, and having procured bits of toilet paper, he wrote down for me the Russian alphabet.

That was my first acquaintance with Cyrillic letters. I then learned some Ukrainian songs and some easy phrases. From time to time the warder asked for volunteers to sweep the floor of the corridor and one day I volunteered in the hope of finding anything useful or interesting in the rubbish. And indeed luck came my way. I found an old Ukrainian newspaper which I furtively hid inside my shirt. This was my textbook for the next few weeks from which, with the help of Vasil and Nicolai, I learned to read Ukrainian.

I was also introduced by them to the poetry of the greatest Ukrainian poet, Taras Gregory Shevchenko. From these beginnings I progressed to the Russian language at a later date. Weeks went by with no change in our situation.

THE SECOND HUNGER STRIKE

The general opinion in the cell was that this time a determined action had to be taken to compel the authorities to speed up 'formalities', as they liked to call the sluggish legal process. Most of us still believed that our detention was a result of some stupid administrative mistake.

We decided again on a hunger strike, this time not to be fobbed off with empty promises. The following morning when the cell door was opened and the coffee urn appeared, we informed the cook that we were on hunger strike. In reply to the inquiry of a senior prison official for the reason of our action, we told him that the Management's promises had been broken and we could no longer endure the dreadful conditions of overcrowding, hopeless waiting and hunger and we demanded a speedy solution to the problem.

Later in the day the prison Governor came at first with further promises, then with threats, but we were determined not to give in. The day passed with no further developments. Under normal conditions fasting a day or two has no harmful effect and can even be beneficial, but when the body had been brought to the verge of starvation, fasting means extreme weakness and mental stress.

The following morning the cell door was opened as usual and the steaming cauldron and trolley with bread rations were rolled right into the cell. This was tantalising. The temptation called for an immense effort to resist. No one retreated from our determined position.

After some twenty minutes the coffee and bread were withdrawn and the cell door was shut. Towards the evening a similar manoeuvre was performed by the prison cook and guards who brought along a steaming urn with soup. Solidarity in the cell was complete and no one moved from one's place.

On the third day of the hunger strike the Deputy Governor came with a guard and pointed to five people, to me among them, who were, according to him, the leaders, and announced that we were going to be shut up in the Kartzer - a punishment cell in Russian. We were led downstairs to the basement into a small room with a little barred window, placed close to the ceiling and without a pane.

It was mid-December and the temperature was below freezing, with the wind blowing through the open window. We were stripped to the waist and shut up in the cell. The problem shifted from hunger to enduring extreme cold. At first we kept moving around in this little cell in an effort to keep warm, but having had no food for two days, we soon became exhausted and we huddled together on the concrete floor. The following day the Deputy Governor came and said that there was no point in going on, that our colleagues in the cell had started eating and it would be foolish for us to continue. We were not impressed by his tale and we repeated our request for an interview with the prosecutor or, at least, to be given permission to write letters to our families. He listened to us attentively and went. We were left with the challenge of enduring the near extreme conditions.

It was impossible to sleep because of the severe cold. The wind was driving in snow between the bars of the open window, the stone floor was biting cold; one could not sit on it longer than a few minutes. On the third day the Governor appeared and promised to allow us to write to our families. This was a minor victory and we felt a sense of achievement. We decided to take food. When back in the cell we were told that no one had broken the fast in spite of cajoling and later threatening with punishment by the Governor. A remarkably solid front despite the variety of people of different nationalities and cultural backgrounds.

We were indeed given each a pencil and a sheet of paper and told to write on one side, leaving the other side for the address. The letters were duly collected, together with all the pencils and we were promised that they would be promptly dispatched. Three weeks went by and none of us had any reply or any confirmation of our letters. It was obvious that we had been tricked.

We were back to square one, helpless and depressed. Unusual thoughts came to my mind. Perhaps life under the Nazis was not all that bad compared with what we were made to experience. Admittedly, Jews were subjected to restrictions, were forced at times to work for the Germans, but at least they were free to move about in their districts and lead a kind of limited free life. I often talked about that with one or two Jewish friends in the cell and they seemed to have had similar thoughts. Little did we know how much Jews were already suffering under German occupation.

One day a young student was brought into our overcrowded cell. He was covered in splotches and was obviously ill. He took off his anorak and put it furtively on the floor in the corner of the cell. A moment later we noticed that the inside of the coat was covered in lice. He looked at us apologetically and nearly cried for shame. The situation was intolerable. Everybody was sorry for the boy, but his presence in the cell could not be tolerated for fear of infection. We knocked at the door and demanded the immediate removal of the boy to the hospital. The guard called his supervisor, who promised some action. Two days later the boy collapsed in high fever and only then was he taken out, presumably, to the prison hospital. The anorak went with him.

Hunger, made more acute by boredom, was gnawing at the stomach and it was difficult to banish the thought of food from your mind. In addition, some people suffered from lack of tobacco, but this problem was to be partly relieved by the event of interrogation.

INTERROGATION

As we found out after some weeks in confinement interrogation sessions always took place late at night, usually after midnight. A double trot in the prison corridor heralded the event. The cover of the spy hole in the door would be raised and a voice calling 'Na bookvoo K!' would be heard, which meant anyone in the cell whose surname began with the letter (bookva) K say Katz, King or Kochubinsky should answer. If the correct name was mentioned, the door would open and a further command would be given, either to follow without one's belongings, which meant an interrogation session, or with belongings which signified a transfer to another cell or to another prison.

At first these late night calls would induce mixed feelings of fear and hope, of apprehension and expectation. There had been rumours that some people had been released hence some flickers of hope would suddenly light up the darkness of your existence.

When taken out from the cell you were ordered to follow the guard without looking sideways or turning your head. This was to prevent seeing prisoners taken out at the same time from other cells. Then followed a walk at a quick pace through interminably long and narrow prison corridors to the door, close to which a specially designed prisoner transport van would be waiting with its back door open. Two armed guards would be standing by. The van had a narrow passage in the middle from which doors led to six cubicles with no windows and no light. The size of a cubicle was only just enough to accommodate a person in the standing position. People with larger shoulders or waists would have to press against the wall.

The journey which probably took only half an hour seemed infinitely long. The destination was a huge, grey building with a multitude of well lit windows. This was the Headquarters of the NKVD (Narodnyi Komisaryat Vnootrennikh Duyel) - the Soviet Secret Police, which later changed into the currently well known KGB.

The van discharged the prisoners one at a time. There was a strict drill: the prisoner from the first cubicle would be led away along the corridor under guard, and when he was about 10 meters away from the van, another prisoner would be taken out, so that no communication between the prisoners should occur. The feeling of isolation was extremely depressing.

I was taken into a sizeable room which was completely empty and had bare walls. It had a barred window which was boarded from the outside and was dimly lit by a bare bulb hanging on a short piece of flex. I was shut in without a word from the guard.

'How long will I be kept here? What will they ask me this time?' I had been interrogated several times before in an office within the walls of the prison, but this time the special journey, the elaborate precautions, the huge building made the occasion seemingly very important. 'Was there anything in what I told them that might have incriminated me?' But my case was very simple: I ran away from the Nazis and I was robbed by them of whatever valuables I had so the Soviet authorities couldn't possibly accuse me of being a 'speculant', someone who came here to do business and cheat the hard working Soviet people.

I had told them on previous occasions that I had been a student and I belonged to no political party, but had some left wing views. 'Shouldn't I have mentioned that?' I wondered. It was difficult to find a reason for their hostility towards me. 'What wrong have I done to deserve that sort of treatment?' It wasn't self-pity that I felt like a wretch. I tried to find a reason, to penetrate the mind of the interrogators, to understand their moral criteria.

My confidence in the integrity of Soviet judiciary had been badly shaken in 1937 when the early leaders of the Party and communist ideologists: Kamieniev, Zinoviev, Radek, Bucharin and others were accused of being spies, and after some well orchestrated trials, summarily shot.

But I could not possibly be equated with them. After all the Soviet Union was the only country in the world where the ideals of socialism were being realised, where various nationalities and races lived in peace and harmony and there were no oppressors or oppressed. 'Am I wrong?' 'Have I worshipped a false god?'

I paced the empty room and agonised under the pressure of

these thoughts. A feeling of helpless, raw, unjustified injury being administered to me was pervading my mind. 'Why are they rejecting my good will, my readiness to serve the cause of freedom, equality and justice, my dedication to the new order where there is no racial prejudice, where the old hate-generating nationalisms were done away with, where there was no bar to the development of one's potential?'

How long I was kept in the 'waiting' room was difficult to estimate. At last I was taken out and led to a large, well lit office, where behind a large desk sat a well groomed and well fed NKVD officer in a smart uniform and of the rank of major. He pointed to a chair at the other side of his desk and began to scrutinise some pages of an already thick pile of hand-written sheets neatly tucked into a folder.

This interrogation session was probably the fourth or the fifth, the first having taken place soon after my arrest. Then the official was a local man, probably an Ukrainian who spoke Polish. Here the interrogator was obviously a high ranking secret police official, a professional at his job. He spoke to me in Russian, of which I had by now a reasonable knowledge. 'Why did you come to the Soviet Union? Who sent you here? How much money did they give you? What sort of sabotage did they ask you to do'?

When I answered to all those questions in the negative, the major would raise his voice and shout threateningly: 'You are a University student - we know that you came here to spy and perform acts of sabotage! You had better confess'!

When I explained that I was Jewish and a refugee from Nazism, that my life was in danger and I simply escaped to save my life - he would say in a menacing voice that I was lying and inventing excuses. At first I was frightened to death, but with time that sort of session became a boring routine and my attention was centred on other things.

In the long corridors leading to the interrogator's office one could almost invariably find some cigarette ends and whoever from our cell, as no doubt, from other cells, was taken along the corridor, had the task to collect as many stubs as possible and bring them to the cell. These would then be opened, the tobacco carefully collected, and using a piece of tissue paper if available or a piece of newspaper, rolled into one cigarette. This would go round, every smoker having a puff or two. Occasionally the interrogator would use the softening technique and offer a cigarette to a prisoner, then there would be a minor holiday in the cell.

My interrogator suddenly changed his voice: from an angry, grating tone to a suave and cultivated manner and gentle sound. He wanted me to tell him more about the situation of Jews in German occupied territories. I told him as much as I knew. Then he said: 'You say you are Jewish, can you speak Yiddish?' I said I could, though not fluently. He then rang his desk bell and in came a man in civilian clothes, looking very Jewish. My interrogator said something to him in a soft voice and then the man asked me in Yiddish to tell him about my escape adventure in Yiddish. I spoke for a few minutes and was listened to attentively. In the course of my narrative, I used the word 'monat' (month) at which point he stopped me and asked what the word meant. I translated it using the Hebrew word 'Chodesh'. That did not satisfy him, and I wondered for a second why. Then I repeated the word pronouncing it slightly differently. I said 'Choidesh' whereupon his face cracked with a fleeting smile of comprehension.

My interrogator, though by now seemingly satisfied with the veracity of my replies, could not refrain from saying: 'What if all you told us is a lie and you turn out to be a 'headyuga' (snake), who came here to harm our Socialist country?!' - to which I did not bother to reply. It was obviously a rhetorical question.

Towards the end of the session he asked me whether I would like to add anything to what I said before. I said: 'Not really, but I have a request'. 'What is it?' he asked. 'Could I be allowed some books to read.' 'Books? Yes, of course'. On leaving the office I had a strange feeling of achievement and was almost grateful to the major for his kindness, having already forgotten the first part of the interview. His promise, as all similar promises by others in the service of the mighty NKVD, never materialised.

COMMUNICATION WITH MY BROTHER, HENRY

The note to my brother that I dropped casually on the way to the Sambor prison miraculously reached him, as I found out much later. Several weeks after my arrest I received a food parcel from Henry. He had great difficulties to find out where I had been taken to, but succeeded and he sent me some food and cigarettes. This was most welcome but it did not last long for the content of the parcel was shared with quite a few. As I discovered later, Henry made tremendous efforts to get me out but was unsuccessful.

Every few weeks the prison doctor used to visit the cell and make a very cursory inspection. He kept a straight face but gave the impression of being sympathetic to our lot. Somehow Henry got to know him and told him about my being inside that prison. It must have been a difficult task for the doctor to find me there but he obviously managed to do so and told Henry in which cell I was kept.

As it happened, opposite my cell window, a short distance away there was a two-storey block of flats. Henry managed to persuade the owner of the flat facing the prison to let him try to see me through the window of one of his rooms opposite my cell. One day the doctor on his visit to our cell whispered to me that my brother would be at the window of the flat opposite the following morning soon after our breakfast. From the floor of the cell one could see only a narrow strip of sky above the boarding of the window. In order to see more one had to be picked up. Two fellow prisoners volunteered. I stood on their shoulders and looked through the strip of window, while a third stood guard at the door with his back to the spy hole. All I managed to do was to wave to my brother and try to smile. He waved back. The next time I saw him was twenty years later.

VOROSHILOVGRAD

A few months later I was in transport to another prison, which, as we discovered, was in the Soviet Ukrainian town, Voroshilovgrad. Though it was extremely difficult to receive any news from outside, rumours were going round about some people having been released and about forthcoming transports to other prisons. These were usually spread by new inmates or by somebody who, when taken out for an interrogation, managed to glean something from what the interrogator said. However, such news, in the majority, was baseless and transports happened unexpectedly.

The usual procedure was a call through the spy hole: 'On the letter X, Y or Z!' and one of those whose surname corresponded was given a short command: 'Get ready with your belongings!'. If several such calls were made we knew that there was going to be a transport to another prison. Of course, you never knew where you were being taken and for how long. The experience of parting with someone one got to know and with whom one had spent months together was sometimes quite painful.

The journey from one prison to another was either by lorries under armed guards or in locked cattle railway carriages. On arrival in a new prison we were usually taken to a large room, ordered to strip completely and to spread our clothes on the floor for easy inspection. Then there followed a strict, undignified, often humiliating body search. The next procedure was registration of names, which meant lining up in front of a small window, the size of a cash point, and waiting your turn to give the name and date of birth to the prison clerk. This usually took hours. Our dossiers, of course, came with us, but that was not enough.

On one occasion the registration clerk must have got fed up with this routine, or perhaps had a sense of humour and most unusually cracked a joke. 'Your name - he asked a prisoner standing in front of the little window? 'Bukowski' (derived from beech), 'Yours?' 'Domb' (oak), 'Yours?' 'Brzozowski' (birch), 'No need to ask' he said to the guard, 'I will put down - a pile of wood.'

THE SMALL CELL IN VOROSHILOVGRAD PRISON

After the search and registration, I was taken into a tiny cell, probably designed only for two, in which there had already been four people. I recognised two of them, whom I noticed in one of the transit camps. They were Jewish, from Poland, apprehended in similar circumstances to mine. The other two were a 16 year old Polish schoolboy and a Russian. As usual the first few hours were spent on exchanging details about the prisons one came from, the length of detention etc., all that with some caution since there was a 'stranger' in the cell.

The 'stranger', Serghiey, turned out to be quite a friendly soul, eager to talk about himself and to listen to others. He befriended the young Polish student, Kaziek, who studied art. There were two narrow bunks at the opposite walls of the cell, and these were already taken by Serghiey and Kaziek, so I and the remaining two slept on the floor. Discomfort is something one can get used to, but what is most difficult is to suppress hunger.

Starvation has a limit beyond which one no longer desires food, one weakens and waits to die, but long stretches of under nourishment banishes every thought from one's mind and concentrates on bread, no other food, just bread. From midday onwards you had to fight the image of the next day's bread ration and it called for a tremendous effort to think of anything else. But it was essential to do so to preserve sanity. And so, when my fellow prisoners discovered that I studied Chemistry at Cracow University, they asked me to teach them some chemistry and physics.

Of course, there were no writing materials of any kind consequently my teaching was restricted to oral expositions and 'writing' simple formulae on the wall with my finger. I recall my thoughts when I explained the movement of a pendulum and wrote invisibly the formula on the wall. I suddenly stopped and shut my eyes. I could see in my mind a timeless pendulum, swinging relentlessly, each swing marking another day, another week, another month of my imprisonment.

How successful my method of teaching was I never discovered but I was asked to carry on for a long period of our staying together in that cell. The presence of Serghiey was at first a mystery to us, but when he began to be called out every few days for long sessions with the prison authorities, it became clear that he was there to report on us. However, by then we knew enough of the system to be careful and to keep away from anything that might conceivably incriminate. Serghiey had been an official at a kolkhoz, had a wife and two children. He told us that the reason for his imprisonment was a disagreement with the higher management, the nature of which he never explained, and as a result of that he was accused of sabotage.

His presence in the cell had its benefits, for every few weeks he would receive a food parcel and some of its contents he would share with fellow prisoners favouring particularly the young student Kaziek. Serghiey seemed to have a paternal feeling towards Kaziek, trying to comfort him and generally showing interest in his welfare. Kaziek offered to sculpt Serghiey's bust and the only available material which might conceivably be suitable for sculpting was...bread. The most precious commodity.

Serghiey, who was still fresh from normal life and not yet affected by the ravages of imprisonment, was in better shape than all of us. However, he must have realised how we would feel if bread was to be wasted and so he resisted the idea for a long time, but then decided to keep a small bit of bread each time he received a food parcel until enough had been accumulated for Kaziek to start on his sculpting job.

Moistened and kneaded, it became malleable and yielded to the skilful hands of the young artist. In a short time the soft, brown material resembling clay, began to acquire the form of a human head and face, and indeed, unmistakably Serghiey's features. The initial feeling of resentment at the waste of precious food gave way to admiration of the piece of art. The finished bust had to be hidden from the eyes of the warder and was occasionally taken out to be looked at.

Apart from my lessons, we had discussions about natural phenomena and one which I remember particularly clearly was on the subject of what causes tides. Serghiey and Kaziek insisted that the rotation of the earth was the reason and my explanation that the moon's attraction causes the phenomenon of tides did not appeal to them at all. We had to agree to differ.

TRANSIT CAMPS (ETAP)

Long distances between detention centres in the vast Soviet Union meant long transports and often unavoidable stops in transit camps. These were old czarist holding camps for political prisoners on their way to Siberia. The Russian revolution aiming at changing the old way of life and destroying the czarist tools of oppression did not, however, do away with the Transit Camps. On the contrary they were now fuller than ever before.

A camp usually consisted of several barracks surrounded by a tall fence with several lines of barbed wire on top and guarded by armed soldiers in watch towers. On arrival to a Transit Camp there followed the ritual personal search and registration. After the search and registration which included finger printing of all fingers, we would be taken in groups to barracks, which were usually large narrow wooden structures with small barred windows. Along the walls there were bare wooden bunks and in some barracks, iron stoves with long flue pipes - one per barrack. In spite of careful precautions the guards were taking to prevent people from one group from making contact with members of other groups, these camps provided opportunities of a degree of communication.

The Transit Camps were a breeding ground for rumours about where they would take us next, what the conditions were going to be in the next camp or prison, new arrests, etc. The crowd was mixed; there were in these camps many Russian criminals and petty thieves who, having been sentenced in courts, were taken to forced labour camps to serve their sentences. In the circumstances theft was rife and advice was given by those in the know to guard one's possessions very carefully. I had very little in my bundle, since most of the things I left home with, had been taken away by the SS men that fatal night in Cracow. I was left with some shirts and some underwear and a most precious possession: a pair of walking boots. These I kept in my bundle which I usually put under my head when lying down to sleep. One would normally not leave anything unattended and it was not easy to make trustworthy friendships in the short time of stay in a Transit Camp to get some help from a friend.

In some camps it was possible to buy tobacco, that is 'krooshki', crushed tobacco stems in the form of bits the size of a grain of rice. These krooshki were rolled into a piece of newspaper, lit and smoked. There apparently was a difference in the taste of a cigarette made using pieces of 'Pravda' and that using 'Izviestie'. Few people had any money and those who managed to get tobacco offered some of it in exchange for bread. In this camp there were prisoners of four nationalities: Poles, Jews, Ukrainians from the occupied Polish territories and Russian convicted criminals, and the tendency was to keep to one's national group.

In one Transit Camp we saw a group of women prisoners,

who were kept on the other side of a wire fence. They seemed to have been less guarded than we were and some came close to the fence and managed to communicate with the men. It was noticeable that those who approached the fence and dared to make contact were Russian or perhaps Ukrainian women. Their behaviour betrayed prison experience, a sort of 'couldn't care less' attitude and even exuberance. Most of them were tattooed and one had on her arm a tattooed sentence 'Zhizn oddam za kharoshooyu yebluyoo' which in plain English means: 'I would give my life for a good fuck'. Stories were going round that some managed to make themselves cylindrical hoses out of a piece of cloth, the size and shape of a penis, and when occasionally hot 'kasha' (groats) was given for dinner fill them with the kasha and use as a tool for sexual gratification.

In the men's barrack there was little evidence of sexual activities; if there were any, and on very rare occasions one could hear some gossip to that effect, these were among the Russian recidivists, who by crook or by hook managed to get more food and consequently were more virile than the rest of us. Conditions in a Transit Camp were usually somewhat more relaxed than in prison, probably because of the size of the barracks and the large numbers of inmates. Here one met a variety of people and some social relations could be established.

A man I got to know well was Albert a dentist from Cracow, intelligent, knowledgeable, fond of music and having a fine singing voice. Normally quite cheerful and sociable.

One morning he appeared to be completely transformed. He was depressingly silent and nervous. At first he would not tell me why he felt like that, but I insisted, whereupon he reluctantly intimated that he forgot the name of his only child. He couldn't sleep all night trying to recall his little daughter's name but in vain. This dreadful amnesia lasted the best part of the day, and when the name suddenly came to his mind, he broke down and cried like a baby. Another young man, approximately my age, with whom I became quite friendly, was Michail, whose family circumstances weren't unlike mine. He left behind parents, a sister and two elder brothers and his mind was often occupied with worries about what might happen to his family. This subject was common to both of us and a particularly close link was forged between us. Next to me on the bunk slept a lecturer of mathematics at the Lvov University, a quiet, rather discrete man, who did not volunteer any information about the reason for his arrest, but who was very pleased to know that I could play chess. He had been arrested relatively recently and somewhat managed to hide a small, collapsible chess set. He was an excellent player and liked to try his skill at blind games, that is, he would turn his back to the chess board and dictate replies to my moves. Only once did I win a game with him.

On one or two occasions he talked to me about the Ribbentrop-Molotov non-aggression pact, expressing critical views about it. It was, of course, paradoxical that a fascist country should suddenly strike up friendship with a communist country. To an objective observer it looked like a true friendship, for it was supported by the export of oil and grain from the Soviet Union to Germany, thus helping her war effort, and enhanced by pro German propaganda which was daily rammed into the Soviet people's throat.

'The rotten capitalist countries (i.e. Britain and France) are doomed to be destroyed and on the ashes of the old regimes a new free world would be created' - that was the official line, and since no other views had ever been allowed to be expressed, some people were convinced that there was some truth in it. The Jews in the cell had no illusions, though no one at the time had the slightest inkling about what the future held for Jews in the occupied territories.

STAROBIELSK

A few days later we found ourselves in a new prison which, as we discovered later, was in Starobielsk, about 200 miles south-east of Voroshilovgrad. After the usual arbitrary division into groups, I was put into a cell which was meant to accommodate 8-10 people and had already 18.

A short time after my arrival eight more were brought into the cell. This, of course, meant that most had to sleep on the floor - a situation by now no longer novel to the Soviet prison population. It was, in fact, preferable to sleep on the floor, for one avoided being in too close contact with other bodies, and since it was by then late spring, it was cooler and more comfortable on the floor. Conditions here were equally bad if not worse, than at the Voroshilovgrad prison.

The daily ration of bread was 300 grams and came with the morning coffee which was a tasteless, often smelly black liquid, hardly drinkable. The small lump of bread was a priceless possession, and if one did not eat it up completely for breakfast, it had to be carefully guarded. But how do you look after a piece of bread in a cell with thirty people, all of whom are hungry? Some could not resist reaching out for an additional piece given the opportunity. And so somebody struck upon the idea of making a bag out of a shirt tail or a vest, attach a string to it, put the bread ration, or what was left of it, inside and carry it round one's neck. But we had neither needles nor cotton and so another fellow prisoner suggested that a needle could be made out of a fish bone by rubbing out an eye in the thick end of the bone with a pebble. Fish bones were in abundance, for our main meal (there were only two a day) which was brought in about 2 PM, was invariably a fish soup, that is, a liquid with a fishy smell and taste and a small piece of fish or several very small pieces which probably resulted from a break up of a larger piece owing to overcooking, floating in it. There were usually sharp bones of various sizes present in the 'soup' and some of them had thick and long, tapering, curved stems terminating in a fine sharp point. These were a suitable material for the manufacture of needles. Michail, tall, heavily built, somewhat clumsy at movements, with a peasant face Ukrainian was exceptionally good with his hands. He easily managed to make several needles out of fish bones, and using one of them, succeeded in pulling out threads from a shirt. Having provided himself with an adequate supply of sewing material, he set up a business of making bread bags. The cost of a bag was half a bread ration, a tremendous price under the circumstances. Later on Michail's enterprise extended to making trunks when the heat in the cell in the height of summer became unbearable.

In spite of the close physical proximity of everybody to everybody else in the cell, it was noticeable that members of the three nationalities, Poles, Jews and Ukrainians did not mix socially. Was it mistrust? or perhaps because of historical reasons? The Ukrainians certainly disliked the Poles and looked upon them as their oppressors, Jews remembered the pogroms at the time of the Ukrainian Hetman Chmielnicki and the sympathetic attitude of the Ukrainians towards Nazi Germany. They had also justified reservations with regard to Poles because of the rise of anti-Semitism in Poland in the thirties. These are of course, generalisations, but under abnormal conditions and severe hardship one loses the critical faculty and patience to discriminate between a good and bad member of a group whose national history was far from being unblemished. Jews had an additional reason to keep to themselves. Their minds were occupied with worries about their families they left behind under the Nazi occupation. There was virtually no knowledge about life in Poland under the Germans, but we Jews had grave forebodings, remembering the vicious Nazi anti-Semitic propaganda.

The overcrowding and hunger were sufficient to break many a weaker constitution, but more acute was the deep feeling of rejection. It was difficult to understand the irrational, completely unjustified hatred of the Soviet authorities to anyone from the West. One felt bitter and helpless, for how could you convince an NKVD officer that you came here as a friend and not a foe? It was difficult to understand why the Soviet Authorities should mistrust Jews who had run away for their lives from the hateful Nazi occupation.

As weeks and months went by any vestiges of good will

towards the Soviet Union I once had evaporated and resentment set in. The question why they do it to friends and supporters rankled in the mind of many people who had belonged to the clandestine Communist Party in Poland, the membership of which, if discovered, carried severe prison sentences.

There were in the cell two men, one in his early thirties, the other probably over fifty, both Jewish, who admitted that they had belonged to the Polish Communist Party. The older one was often in tears, not being able to comprehend that a man like him, who had worked for the Party all his adult life, disregarding the danger of imprisonment, should now be incarcerated by the very authorities in whom he placed his trust, to whom he looked all his life for the fulfilment of his hopes of a better, more just future. The other, tall, thin, with a ready, if somewhat, sardonic smile, confided that he had spent two years in Bereza Kartuska under suspicion of having been a Communist. Bereza Kartuska was a Concentration Camp in Poland, established some years before the war by the Government which, after the death of Marechal Pilsudski in 1935, became increasingly reactionary and anti-Semitic.

The purpose of the Camp was to detain without trial all those, who, in the eyes of the Authorities, that is usually the Police, were an undesirable element. The decision was arbitrary and there was no appeal. The victims were largely members of the Polish Socialist Party, and those who were suspected of being communists. There was no racial discrimination. The regime in the Camp was extremely rigorous and there was no fixed time limit for detention.

In the early thirties, when I was still at school, Jewish youth in their late teens and early twenties usually belonged to one of the two political groups: Zionist and Socialist anti-Zionist. The Zionists were catered for by a few organisations, covering the political spectrum from the right wing Revisionists or Betar, whose leader was Vladimir (Zeev) Zhabotinsky, through the middle, Hanoar Hazioni, to the left, Hashomer Hatzair. The anti-Zionist Socialists belonged to either the Bund, which had a friendly association with the PPS (Polish Socialist Party) and was thought of in historical terms as the Second International, and the illegal Communist Party.

The Communists, a much smaller group, had no formal organisation and consisted of a small number of intellectuals and a somewhat larger number of working people, Jews and non Jews, with the predominance of the former. The activities of the Communists were clandestine and usually amounted to small meetings at which Marxism was discussed, illegal literature was read and some very modest forms of demonstration on the 1st of May were planned. This was usually restricted to putting out a red flag on a balcony or top of a roof.

For any of these activities, if caught in the act or detected, the 'guilty' was liable to from 3 to 5 years in prison. David Khenchinski, now about 30, thoughtful and intellectual, had served a 5-year sentence in Poland for running a Communist cell. In spite of the present circumstances, in spite of deprivation and the glaring, cynical injustice, he remained a true believer in Soviet Communism. His faith was unshaken and the imprisonment he ascribed to a 'temporary administrative aberration'. There were days when his spirit flagged, but his convictions never seemed to lose their strength. At times he gave the impression of having a mystical desire to expiate for the crime of the oppressors, a form of flagellation.

I told him that I had once strong radical views and great sympathies for the Soviet Union, but I changed my views in 1937, at the time of the infamous trials of the Communist leaders, who were falsely accused of spying for Germany. This did not change his mind; it obviously wasn't a question of reasoning, it was a deep-rooted emotion, a tragic case of rejected love.

The hot summer days in the congested cell were dragging on interminably. However, one morning, to our great surprise, a warder came along and announced that if we wished we could borrow books from the prison library. This was the first time for nearly nine months of my detention that books were allowed into the cell. The selection was extremely limited and very few inmates could read Russian. The only book with large print and easy language was the 'History of the Communist Party', presumably, a special edition for beginners or under-educated, and that was what I chose to read. I found it easy to read and I was asked to read it aloud. This filled the time for some days and was a considerable relief from boredom. Another form of collective activity were exercises carried out under instructions of a fellow prisoner, an ex-PE teacher. He explained to us that if we didn't stretch our limbs, our muscles would atrophy and he was so persuasive that we all obeyed his command and did the exercises he conducted.

Because of lack of room we were divided into two groups. Touching toes, moving arms, turning one's head, crouching, etc., had to be performed in silence, so as not to arouse the suspicion of warders. It was sometimes difficult to suppress laughter at the efforts of some of the inmates.

Nearly a whole year had passed and I still did not know what I was accused of, what crime I had committed. I knew nothing of how my family was getting on under German occupation. I had pangs of conscience for having run away and leaving my parents, sisters and a brother in a hostile environment. 'Was my present position a punishment for my cowardice and selfishness? Why didn't I share the fortune of the rest of my family?' These thought were always in the back of my mind and often filled me with remorse. I often thought of my father, who, in the last two years before the outbreak of the war had been rapidly declining, had a very low emotional threshold and was often tearful. How is he now? Can he stand up to the difficult war conditions? Little did I know how terrible those conditions became for the Jewish population. My mother held a very special place in my heart. She was the kindest woman I have ever known: quiet, hard working, undemanding, caring and loving, but also having a sense of humour and using it to relieve tension when, at times, family difficulties arose. 'Is my brother allowed to work? How do my two sisters fare?' These thoughts recurred time and again, but one felt completely helpless, not being able to get any news from anywhere.

THE SENTENCE

The frequency of interrogation sessions diminished and only occasionally someone would be called out from our cell, usually after midnight, for a period of two or three hours. There was no longer any interest in what 'they' wanted to know; the question directed to the colleague prisoner returning from the interview was how many cigarette stubs he managed to collect from the corridors of the NKVD building. Towards the end of the fifth month I and some of the inmates were taken out from the cell and put into a smaller cell.

A fortnight later the prison Governor and his Deputy came into the cell and handed out a slip of paper the size of a normal envelope to each of us. In my case it read as follows: 'You have been sentenced to three years in a Corrective Camp (Eespravitelneey Lagher) for crossing the border illegally', signed: 'Emergency Court in Moscow'.

Sentences ranged from 3 to 8 years. None of us appeared in Court, had a proper case made out, had an opportunity to call witnesses, to defend oneself, or given the right of appeal. We were stunned. Three, five, eight years detention, for what?!

A middle aged man from the Polish town Radom, a shop keeper, uninterested in politics, worrying most of the time about his family, kind and friendly, received 5 years. He broke down and cried like a child. David Khenchinski, a confirmed communist, who spent some years in a Polish prison for his convictions, received 8 years! Madness? or perversion and irony?

The aftermath of the Spanish Civil War came to one's mind. After the defeat of the International Brigade by Franco's Forces some of the members of the Brigade managed to go to Russia. They were promptly arrested and sent to forced labour camps.

Evidently the Soviet Authorities despised foreign communists; in fact, they were afraid that the true communist ideology of the foreigners might weaken the absolute dictatorship of the Soviet Communist Party. Thus, those among us who professed to be communists fared much worse than others: their sentences were invariably more severe.

A few days later we were taken to a Transit Camp from where prisoners were sent to their destination. We were not told to which labour camp we were being taken. In a way it was a relief to know that the stupid, tedious interrogation sessions were over. The conditions in prison were so debilitating that any change had a promise of improvement, or so we thought.

JOURNEY TO THE FORCED LABOUR CAMP

A strange feeling of apathy pervaded everybody. 'Does it really matter where one is being taken?' By then I had completely lost faith in the capacity of the Soviet Authorities to exercise any sort of justice. Their cynicism had become so obvious that no rational criteria could possibly be applied to their actions. There were about 40 people in each cattle railway truck, which had two tiers of bunks with no bedding of any kind. High above the upper bunk, on both sides of the iron sliding door, there were two small windows, approximately sixty cm by thirty cm, covered with close bars from outside. In the middle of the truck, between the bunks there was a small hole in the floor serving as a toilet.

We were taken by lorries under the guard of armed soldiers to a railway siding where we were divided arbitrarily into groups and ordered into the trucks. Those who got in first managed to occupy places near the windows, the rest of us - wherever we could. The arbitrariness of division often meant the loss of a friend. If that happened a feeling of loneliness set in and one was again among strangers.

The train, composed of twenty five or thirty trucks, started on its long journey to the far North. How long the journey would take none of us prisoners knew, neither did we know our destination. In prison there was a routine: the day was divided into two parts and the important events breaking up the time were the morning coffee and bread ration and the second daily meal in the early afternoon, whereas now, in these claustrophobic conditions no foreknowledge existed about what or when anything might take place. Food was delivered irregularly and at increasingly longer intervals. It consisted of a loaf of bread for six people, and occasionally, some pieces of herring. No cooked meal or beverage of any kind was given to us. The train rumbled along for days, stopped at places to be shunted onto different tracks and the only noticeable change was a steady drop in temperature and an increase in the layer of 'frost' deposited on the inner walls of the carriage. This 'frost' turned out to be most useful for it was a substitute for water which we were refused, out of malice or perhaps because of shortage in the increasingly colder regions of the far North. Speculation was rife as to the destination and conditions in the camp to which we were being taken. 'Eespravitelneey Lagher' means 'corrective camp', but what substance does this name describe? Drill, discipline, what sort of existence may we expect in it? No one knew and no one would have guessed.

ZHITH BOODESH

It must have been already a fortnight since we were herded into the cattle trucks and carted North to the camp, when another of those barbed wire fenced and watch tower guarded transit camps became our home for two days. After the usual procedure of stripping to the skin for inspection and queuing up for registration, though our documents came with us and there could not have been the slightest possibility of any changes in the number of prisoners in transport, there followed another procedural event. We were lined up in front of what turned out to be a surgery for a medical examination.

The queue in front of me moved fairly quickly and shortly I found myself inside a small room with bare walls, in one corner of which there were a table and two chairs. At the far side of the table there were two women, one sitting, the other standing; both had stethoscopes round their necks. One was quite young, probably middle or late twenties, the other who was sitting at the table with a pen in hand, was nearer fifty. The sight of clean, neatly dressed and healthy looking women was almost a revelation. For a moment I had a feeling that life was perhaps returning to normal.

A tiny fleeting current of hope ran through my brain when suddenly a sharp order came from the young woman doctor: 'Undress completely!' I was not sure whether I understood the order and asked what to do. The doctor looked at me, smiled and repeated the instruction. I felt awful. To strip myself naked in front of two women in broad daylight - I could not make myself do it. I hesitated. 'Now, come on' she urged me in a friendly voice. I reluctantly obeyed. The examination was perfunctory and lasted only a minute or two. Encouraged by her friendly attitude, I asked her what the camp we were going to was like and she answered laconically, still smiling benignly: ' Zith boodesh, no yebath ne zakhotches'- the equivalent of which in English would be:' You will live, but you will have no urge to fuck'. I was slightly shocked by the outspokenness of that woman, but perfectly understood the situation.

The transport rumbled on for another week. Day and night merged into an amorphous timelessness, seemingly without end, but when the end of the journey came, there was little excitement.

Exhaustion, cold and starvation made us all apathetic. It was night and a severe frost when the doors of the carriages were unlocked and slid open with a squeaking noise and the prisoners were discharged onto the railway platform to face a row of guards with rifles, among whom there were a number with Alsatian dogs.

We were ordered to line up in fours and a senior officer with two helpers started counting the rows. Soon the whole transport was divided into groups which were then separated and each group, guarded by armed soldiers, was ordered to follow an officer. The division was arbitrary.

THE FORCED LABOUR CAMP, CHIBIU (KOTLAS)

We were sufficiently numb not to have any strong feelings. A state of passivity ensued, and surrounded by a number of armed guards, we followed the officer. The slow march over snow- covered frozen tracks lasted several hours. At last the contours of a high fence with barbed wire and watch towers came into sight. Outside the narrow gate leading to the camp were already assembled two rows of armed soldiers. The column narrowed to a single row to enable the officials at the inside of the gate to count us. In the darkness of the late winter night the outlines of long barracks were only just discernible. When the counting was over, we were led into a dimly lit barrack in which were already many prisoners. A casual gesture of the officer towards one part of the barrack indicated our living space. There were two tier bunks made of unplaned logs with no bedding of any description and there appeared to be no windows. A single kerosene lamp hanging in the middle of the barrack grudgingly offered some light which was just enough to find one's way along the passage between the rows of bunks. In the middle of the barrack there was a large wood burning stove provided with a flue pipe which had a long horizontal section before it turned at right angle upwards and out through the roof.

Carrying my bundle of clothes I looked round and to my surprise and delight, I noticed Michail, whom I had met at one of the transit camps and with whom I had struck up a friendship. The first thing he said to me was to look carefully after my possessions because there was a lot of stealing going on. He then told me something about the composition of the camp population. The majority were people from that part of Poland which the Soviet Union had invaded in 1939, but there was a substantial number of Russian prisoners who had been in the camp a long time. Some of these were hardened criminals who considered themselves to be the aristocracy of the camp. They usually occupied the best places in the barrack and they managed to provide themselves with some sort of bedding and blankets and congregated close to the stove. They looked upon us as intruders and took every opportunity to steal everything worth having.

My bundle contained two shirts, two pairs of pants, three pairs of socks, a sweater and the mentioned earlier precious pair of brown walking boots which I begrudged myself using - hoping to enjoy it when freed. I carried my bundle with me whenever I moved from my bunk and only on rare occasions when I got to know my neighbour well, did I entrust it to his care. This, of course, was by mutual arrangement. The morning revealed the reality of the camp. A half a dozen large wooden huts with 2 ft. by 2 ft. windows in one of the longer walls and a door at one end, spread over an area of perhaps 2 to 3 acres. Round the perimeter was a tall wooden fence with barbed wire on top and watch towers at the four corners, with armed guards. Several smaller wooden buildings, one near the gate, drew my attention. These, as I was informed, were occupied by the camp doctor, by the management, and the one at the gate, by the guards.

After a rather informal 'wake up' signal we were told to make our way to the cook house for our morning coffee. We were not given any containers and it was left to one's ingenuity to acquire utensils of any sort. We had each a wooden spoon and this was looked after carefully; some of the 'new' inmates managed to borrow from the 'old' ones some sort of vessel. I and quite a few others had no idea how to go about this problem. Michail told me that one way was to buy a pot from a Russian prisoner and he put me in touch with that entrepreneur. This fellow had been in the camp for a number of years and had developed a business in old rusty pots which he sold to newcomers, not for money but for a vest, a pair of socks or pants. There were two kinds of tins, with and without wire handles, the former naturally, fetched a higher price. With the coffee there came a portion of black bread. Life looked quite good.

No further orders were given and only much later in the day the new arrivals were told that we would be led to the doctor for an examination. The doctor's house was a small wooden shed with two rooms, a waiting room and a 'surgery', both bleak and almost empty apart from a long bench in the waiting room and a little table and a wooden stool in the 'surgery'. The 'medical' was a quick one, an assessment made by visual inspection, the purpose of which was allocation to two kinds of work: felling trees and clearing sites, that is, removing snow from the site to provide easy access to the trees marked for felling, and after a tree was felled, to dig out its root.

I was allocated to the latter type of work. We were then issued with clothes, which consisted of a 'foofayka' - a sort of anorak, cotton wool padded trousers and a pair of rubber shoes (not boots) - all three items had been used before and were in need of repair. There was a remarkable degree of freedom of movement between barracks, which after prison life, appeared to be quite a change for the better. We were left in peace for three days to recover after the long journey. One had a mixed feeling of anxiety and relaxation, for there seemed to be no one over us. But this was soon dispelled when on the second day some officials came into the barrack and an order was given to line up. Names were called out and a division was made into 'brigades'.

My 'brigade' was a site-clearing and a stump-uprooting one, led by a Russian 'koolak' of about fifty, called Strelok. 'Koolak' is a derogatory name given to a farmer who did not immediately agree to collectivisation and often, rather than passing on his cattle to the kolkhoz, slaughtered it. Koolaks were rounded up in the late twenties and early thirties and severely punished: some by shooting, others by long sentences in forced labour camps. A position of brigadier was a considerable privilege and carried substantial benefits, one of which, and perhaps the most important, was the possibility of having warm and sound, felt boots, and the other, a safe, standard meal. People were fed according to the amount of work performed. Food was divided into three categories: 1st, 2nd and 3rd 'kotiel' (pot). Those who completed the allocated quota received the 2nd, those who exceeded the quota got the 3rd and those who under performed - the 1st. The 2nd 'pot' was the standard one and consisted of 400 grams of black bread, morning coffee and evening meal, usually soup with a small piece of fish or meat floating in it. The 1st had its bread reduced to 200 grams and a very thin soup with nothing in it. What the 3d 'kotiel' was like I never discovered, for no one in my brigade, nor anyone of the non-Russian inmates I got to know, ever had the privilege of having this coveted meal. This was reserved for the 'Stakhanovites', that is, the exceptionally good workers, who, as it happened, were invariably Russian old timers.

How they achieved higher than quota results was a mystery to us but in time we learned the secret.

The 'relaxed' time was over on the third day. On the fourth day, in the early, still dark morning a roll call and a sharp order to line up in front of the bunks for a 'provierka' (counting) was given. This process lasted exceptionally long because, on the second count to check the first, the total differed, and so a third counting was carried out with presumably satisfactory results. This became a daily procedure. Morning coffee over, a call for joining individual brigades was made and a brisk march to the tool shed followed. Axes and shovels were handed out and the column, four in a row, followed the Brigadier into the forest. The armed soldiers, one in the front, the other in the back of the column marched with us, but before we set out, the one at the back gave a warning in a loud voice: 'shug iv pravo, shug iv leavo, prinimayou roozhie bez predooprezhdenia!' which means 'a step to the right, a step to the left, I shall shoot without warning'.

Snow was two to three feet deep and the temperature well below freezing. Soon we walked through the forest and the depth of snow was increasing. Dawn was breaking when we arrived at the place where we were ordered to stop. The brigadier, Strelok, marked out an area to be cleared of snow and another where trees had already been felled and where stumps had to be dug out. Strelok was a quiet, even kindly man, but in fear of losing his position, he insisted that work should be carried out according to plan. The work was hard and unless one got on with it continuously, one suffered from acute cold. We were allowed to light a 'kostior' - a bonfire, but the time spent at it was strictly regulated: a few minutes every two hours, and a little longer lunch time when one consumed the rest of the bread ration.

Strelok's philosophy was simple and sound: 'If you want to

survive, work to earn your food, for in the camp there is no alternative. We worked 8 to 10 hours a day, which in winter meant leaving the camp in complete darkness. On returning to the barrack the most important event was the distribution of the bread ration and the collecting of one's dinner. The Brigadier's important task, apart from supervising the work was to do the paperwork, that is, to work out who performed the quota and was entitled to a full bread ration and who was not. After he had done that, he collected the bread portions from the well guarded storehouse and brought them along to the barrack, together with 'talons', that is, tickets that one had to hand in at the cookhouse window to get dinner. The distribution of bread was naturally eagerly awaited, and when received, there ensued within oneself a tremendous struggle: whether to consume the lot or to retain some for the following day. A 2nd 'pot' dinner was reasonably satisfying and capable of stifling the call for food for a couple of hours. However, the nagging feeling of hunger soon reasserted itself, particularly after hard work in the open. 'Man does not live by bread alone' - how hollow this biblical saying would have sounded in the circumstances we found ourselves?

It is a myth that starvation ennobles, that it transposes one onto a higher spiritual plane. Imposed prolonged starvation drains one dry of thoughts and feelings except the desire of food. The persistent, painful suction at the stomach dulls normal sensitivity to the environment and lowers human dignity.

In the first few weeks I felt so exhausted that after my evening meal I could do nothing except drag myself to my place on the upper bunk and lie down half asleep. Many of the newcomers behaved in a similar fashion, and since there was a tendency for us to stick together, almost half of the barrack appeared to be dead in the unusually early hours of the evening.

The slumber was broken later, probably between 9 and 10 o'clock (no one knew the exact time for no watches were available) by the guards ordering to line up for the interminable and dreaded 'provierka'. Only after that one could go to 'bed', which meant taking off one's clothes and using them as some kind of bedding. I used to fold my trousers and pat then under me, and cover myself with my anorak. With time one developed a degree of resistance to fatigue and was able to spend some time on other activities apart from sleeping.

There were no washing facilities, and in order to keep reasonably clean I used handfuls of snow to wash my face and hands. One of the plagues of life in a Soviet forced labour camp was the abundance of lice and bugs, but the management had a solution to this problem. Every camp was provided with a 'voshoboika' (a lice killing chamber). This was a small, windowless room attached to the communal bath, to which a party of inmates used to be taken once a fortnight for a shower. The small room would be filled with steam and our clothes placed on racks inside, while we were having a shower. Lice cleverly hide themselves in the seams where they are well protected and where they safely lay their eggs.

The steaming out process was hardly ever effective; much more radical measures were required to fight this scourge. That is when the long, hot flue pipe came in to play a most vital role. After dinner, if one managed to muster enough strength, the ritual of burning out lice from the seams of one's shirt began. If one succeeded to get a place at the pipe, which was never easy, off came the shirt and pants and after turning them inside out, their seams would be run over the hot pipe. If pops could be heard one knew that the job had been done properly.

A conversation I had one evening with a Russian inmate about life in the capitalist countries, of which he knew nothing except what Soviet propaganda told him, ended with his posing the question: 'oo vas voshoboika yest? - do you have a lice killing chamber?' 'No', I said. 'Kataya oo vas kooltoora?!' 'Where is your culture?!' he exclaimed indignantly.

In the very short Arctic summer, in addition to the plague of lice there was an onslaught of mosquitoes and bugs; why the latter should be particularly active in summer I do not know. Mosquitoes attacked people as well as horses, the viciousness of attack could be gauged by the rate at which the body of a mosquito changed shape and colour from the initial small and black frame to a pink and finally red balloon, many times its normal size. In this state the insect is heavy and clumsy. In spite of the pain some people allowed mosquitoes to feed on their body, and when the insect had its fill, its life would be terminated by a blow. Thus vengeance was wreaked on the voracious bloodsucker.

THE 'SURGERY'

The 'doctor' who ran the Surgery was not a qualified doctor; he was a paramedic, who had had a few years experience as a male nurse in a hospital. He was Polish, but had lived in the Soviet Union for some years before the war. The story as told to me was that he was a communist and went to Russia to live according to his convictions, but his ideals soon appeared to the authorities a heresy and he was arrested, as so many other communists-idealists had been, and sentenced to ten years in a forced labour camp. He was very lucky to be given the job of camp doctor, for that was a most privileged position, carrying the benefit of good camp clothes, valenkys (warm felt boots), most probably top ration food, and above all, a warm and reasonably clean hut. His position gave him the power to bestow upon a patient the blessing of sick leave for a maximum of three days. However, he had to be very careful lest he be accused of sabotage, and so, unless one had a high temperature, the bonus of staying in was unattainable. I was unlucky in that respect. Though I often felt very tired, I never developed a high temperature; consequently I was out at work every day during my 8 months in camp, except on New Year's day, the one of the only two days holiday a year, the other being the 7th of November - commemorating the Revolution.

There were cases of self mutilation in order to stay away from work. Of course, if discovered that the injury was self

82

inflicted, an additional sentence of 3, 5 or more years would inevitably follow.

THE CAMP ARISTOCRACY

The majority of inmates in the Cheebue camp consisted of people from the newly invaded territories, but there was a substantial number of Russian prisoners, some of whom were serving very long sentences even by Soviet standards. A fifteen or twenty year sentence was not unusual and these people looked upon us as being lower species. A three year sentence was considered a 'dgietzkyi srok', a childish sentence, which, as one said to me, 'you could sit out on the lavatory seat'. Among them were recidivists for whom camp life had been the only one they knew. This, they reasoned, gave the right to a more comfortable life than others and they did everything possible to achieve their goal.

They had their own brigades and they invariably managed not only to fulfil their quota but to achieve a surplus, a 'Stakhanovite' measure, which entitled them to the top ration and very often, to a monetary bonus, something like a rouble a week. Felling trees without power assisted tools, just with a saw and an axe, is a very arduous task. The felled tree had to be cleared of all branches, then cut up into 10 feet long logs, out of which a stack of the required height was then built. The branches had to be burnt and the site left clean. This was a Herculean task, impossible to perform by the team in the time allocated.

However, the Russian teams were always successful and the

secret how they managed to do it was revealed to me by chance. The stack of timber had the correct dimensions and the inspector, who daily turned up to measure the stacks, entered the figures into the camp record book. What he did not know, or chose not to know, was that the middle of the stack was empty.

The cumulative effect of under nourishment took its toll. Most people became lethargic, some suffered from diarrhoea and loss of weight was quite general. Only those who managed to supplement their rations by hook or by crook kept up their strength. Those were usually Russian long term prisoners. There was a strange morality in their behaviour: theft was perfectly acceptable, particularly of public property but also anything from other inmates, especially from 'foreigners'. But they drew a strict line which they never crossed. They would not steal the bread ration. One wandered what was the source of that moral barrier. Though the Russian recidivists were better off than most of us, some of them succumbed to the effect of lack of vitamin 'A', which manifested itself in 'night-blindness'. One could not help deriving satisfaction, a sort of Schadenfreude from the fact that a zhulik, a ruthless criminal, who threw his weight about during the day, stole and behaved disgracefully to the weaker kind, was suddenly struck by a weakness and depended on other people's help. While 'night blindness' affected a few, scurvy was the scourge of many. There was hardly anyone who did not suffer from bleeding gums, and subsequent loss of teeth. There was no vitamin 'C' in the camp diet and there was virtually no way to provide the body with the necessary vitamin. A feeble attempt was occasionally made by the doctor by handing out at the 'surgery' a few small, raw potatoes which supposedly were to provide some vitamin 'C'. The effect was minimal.

The winter was hard. The snow was three feet deep and the temperature 35 degrees below zero. The main concern was survival, which meant trying everything possible to get enough food to avoid catastrophic weight loss and fatal disease. Quite a few failed in that effort and wasted away. Some could not resist the temptation to search for food in the rubbish heap in which the best one could find were rejected fish heads and rotten cabbage leaves. One day a rumour went round that the camp Superintendent's cat disappeared and it wasn't difficult to guess that it ended up as a welcome food supplement for some of the more enterprising inmates.

MY 'FRIEND' ILYA

As I later discovered my brother, Henry, whom I fleetingly saw through the window of my prison cell in Sambor, made a great effort to get me released from prison. He persuaded a class mate of mine, Rashka Zayonchkovska, who happened to be in Lvov, to make a declaration to the authorities that she was my wife and request my relief on compassionate grounds. There had been cases of release on such grounds but this stratagem did not work in my case. And so Henry decided to trace my movements which must have been a tremendous task given the secretiveness and unapproachability of the Soviet Judiciary and administrative authorities. It was one of the greatest surprises in my life when one winter evening after my return from work, I was called to the camp office and told that there was a parcel for me, which would be handed over to me after inspection. I wasn't told who it was from and I wasn't shown it. My curiosity was roused to a pitch and I could hardly wait to take possession of it. Much later I was called again to the office and handed an open brown paper parcel with a few items in it. On the outside was Henry's handwriting, that is, the address of the camp, and on the other side, only his name.

The items were about a pound of sugar in lumps, a piece of lard, a piece of soap and about 30 cigarettes spread loosely in the parcel. I was also given a ten rouble note and five single roubles which, they said, came together with the parcel. It was quite obvious that half of the stuff was missing, however I was very happy to have some sign of life from Henry. If only I could communicate with him, but that was out of the question. No camp prisoner had ever been allowed to communicate with the outer world. My joy was mixed with worry how to protect the precious goods from theft and above all, where to keep the money, for this sum of money constituted a fortune in camp conditions. A rouble would buy two pounds of bread, that is as much bread as a good camp 'worker' would get for two and a half days. In effect it meant that with careful husbandry I could supplement the ration for many weeks and stop being hungry. What a marvellous turn of fortune! The usual way of carrying money in a bag on a string round one's neck proved not only unsafe but downright dangerous, for there had been cases of injury caused by a sudden 'money' bag pull off. I therefore decided to keep the single roubles for immediate use and to hide the ten rouble note in the seam of my anorak. I discreetly and carefully undid part of the lining of the left shoulder, inserted the note and stitched up the lining. Since I never parted with the anorak I was satisfied that the money was secure.

I intended to change it at a later date. The piece of lard and the sugar I wrapped up in a rag and hid the object in snow behind the barrack. I did not tell anyone what happened in the last day or two except Michail with whom I shared the provision, cigarettes etc. There ensued a period of abundance. Every evening after work I made my way to the laryok, the camp shop, where I purchased a pound of bread which Michail and I consumed voraciously with our evening soup. The transformation from a state of continuous hunger robbing one of the ability to concentrate on anything else but food to a position in which one could gratify the demands of one's stomach was quite dramatic.

Things looked quite rosy. The snow was no longer as deep as before, the frost did not bite as severely as it had done and there was hope for a better future. We managed even to smile occasionally and to notice some funny sides of camp life. This state of bliss came to an end all too quickly. One morning I was shocked to find that the seam of my anorak was cut open on the outside and the money was missing. This was a devastating blow. There was no point in lodging a complaint with the camp authorities, for I knew from other people's experience that it would lead to nothing. I could not even mention the fact to anyone for I kept the whole business secret and Michail the only one I longed to talk to, had already departed with his brigade to work.

That evening after dinner I had an unusual visitor. In the neighbouring barrack there lived the 'chief' of the recidivists, a six foot three tall Russian, lean and strong like a horse, serving a 15 year sentence. He was normally quite civil, had a powerful bass baritone and played the balalaika.

His name was Ilya. I was resting on the bunk when I heard a friendly shout: 'Comrade, how are you?' Taken by surprise I did not answer at once and looked at him quizzically. He smiled and said: 'You look very worried, is there anything wrong with you?' I did not know what to say, but he did not really expect an answer. 'I know what happened', he said. 'You lost your money. Do you know who took it?' he asked rhetorically, and not waiting for my reaction, he continued: 'I took it. And do you know why? Because you were using your money wrongly. You were spending it on black bread which is no good for your health. You were eating it, but in fact, it was eating you' he added philosophically. 'I want to show you how you should have used your money. Tonight there wiil be a party in my barrack. I bought white flour, milk and fat and am baking blinies (known otherwise as blintzis) all for your money, and I am inviting you to the party.'

I was dumbfounded and did not know what to say, 'No doubt', he carried on, 'you want to know how I knew where the money was. Well, I'll tell you. When lying on your bunk you kept touching your left shoulder every so often, which made me think that you were checking on a hidden treasure and of course, I was right'. He repeated the invitation and left. My anger receded. After a while I realised that I rather liked the fellow and I decided to go to the party. That evening there was a small gathering in Ilya's barrack round his 'bed', which was a much more comfortable bunk than the usual. The bunk was covered with a piece of white cloth and in the middle there was a small pile of hot blinies, the sort of food I had not seen for ages. Ilya handed out one to every participant of the occasion, informing then who was the 'benefactor'. After the feast he took his balalaika, sat down and began to sing a traditional Russian song. Some joined in. The scene was extraordinary and completely incongruous with the environment. I forgot the harm done to me and enjoyed what at the time appeared to me, a warm and friendly atmosphere.

THE CAMP OFFICE

The business of the camp office consisted of checking the work output and allocating bread and soup 'talons' to the several work brigades. These 'talons' were the life sustaining agents. Withholding them as punishment for poor work or for any other reason meant starvation which, if prolonged, resulted in many cases in death. In the office there worked two men, one Pole and one Russian.

The Pole, Vladislav Ruszala, middle aged, slightly stooping, but showing signs of comfortable upbringing and good education, befriended me and liked to talk to me whenever an opportunity arose. He was, however, somewhat careful, lest people would suspect too close a friendship between us. He was a primary school teacher in Lvov and was arrested together with a large number of 'intelligenzia' and sent to camp. That was all he told me about his case and I did not ask for details.

There was probably little more to tell because his uninteresting case, completely deprived of drama, was one of thousands. What he mostly dwelt on was his family, his wife and two children. He found some relief in recalling to me his close family life, the love of his work and the loss of his friends. Occasionally he would slip into my hand a talon, which would provide me with an additional soup. This godsend gift I used to share with Michail, who badly needed some extra food since he hardly ever completed his quota. He was put into a tree felling team which meant extremely hard work under most arduous conditions. He was slightly built and the many months in prison drained his strength. He consistently used to receive half of the normal bread ration. The sporadic little extra food could do little to improve his condition, consequently he became lethargic and carried on in a state of resignation and hopelessness.

I was luckier than Michail. I was assigned to a snow clearing and stump uprooting team which entailed clearing an area for the team of tree fellers, and after the latter completed their task, our team would dig out the stumps and level the ground.

The amount of our work depended on the efficiency of the tree fellers, and since they hardly ever fulfilled their quota, we managed to be on the credit side, with the result that our 2nd 'pot' was always secure.

The Russian clerk from the camp office, Serghiey Ivanovich, was about fifty, tall and thin, wearing glasses and a worried expression on his face. He would emerge from his office in the late evening hours and walk the distance of 100 meters or so between the kitchen and his office. I met him through Mr. Ruszala. At first he showed no interest in talking to me but after some weeks, he became more friendly and open. He trusted me with his views about the Soviet Government and Stalin.

He was an official in a Kolkhoz, he had worked hard and

was honest (he assured me). One day, out of the blue, he was arrested, accused of sabotage and of being an enemy of the people and sentenced to 10 years forced labour. He was full of venom about the authorities and very pessimistic about the future. I listened sympathetically to his talk but thought it better to be careful since I could not be sure whether he was genuine or perhaps an agent provocateur. Serghiey Ivanovich had also access to soup talons in the office and he also handed out clandestinely some to trusted friends, but not without anything in return: a vest, a pair of socks or pants would get you two or three talons. But this could only happen with relative newcomers, since the supply of vests, socks etc. was extremely limited and became quickly exhausted.

Half of the bread ration collected in the evening would be consumed with the evening meal and the rest put in a bag made of a shirt tail, provided with a string and carried round one's neck. Though the Russian inmates would not steal bread, 'our' own people could not always be trusted. On arrival at the site in the forest, after issuing instructions of what to do, the Diesiatnik, that is the 'Brigadier', would put on a bonfire, and while warming his back, would keep an eye on the workers.

There was always an armed guard who usually took up a strategic position a few steps away to have a better view of everybody. About midday we were allowed to approach the fire in two's, put the bread on the end of a stick, toast it at the fire and consume it. There was a shortage of tobacco and smokers suffered from it very acutely. It was sometimes possible to buy a glassful of tobacco chips (krooshki), that is, small pieces into which a tobacco leaf stalk had been cut, and roll a quantity of these pieces into a scrap of newspaper and smoke. But the only people who had money to purchase this 'tobacco' were some of the Russian inmates. The supply was very short and very sporadic. Some addicted smokers would offer a portion of their bread ration for a small quantity of 'krooshki'.

But there was another, albeit very rare source of much more superior tobacco than 'krooshki'. The camp had occasionally been visited by high officials whose life style was miles different from not only that of the inmates but also that of the commandant and his helpers. Those well-to-do people, who smoked normal, 'packeted', good quality cigarettes, would at times discard half smoked cigarettes. These stubs were treasures. When found by an inmate, a stub would be carefully opened, and used to produce the well known from prison 'practice' way; a cigarette smoked with relish, usually by more than one person.

Matches, as everything else, were in very short supply and one learned to divide a match into two halves, and with skill, into four workable matches. The inventiveness and skill of some inmates went further than that, and made it possible to become independent of the provision of matches. A small piece of steel, say from a broken file or rasp, a pebble of flint and a piece of cotton wool from one's anorak provided adequate equipment for producing effective red heat to light a cigarette. The technique was not simple and a fair amount of practising was required to achieve a positive result.

You placed a swab of cotton wool on the ground, bent over it with the piece of steel in one hand and the flint in the other and struck the flint with the metal such that the produced spark landed on the wool and started the process of smouldering. Then one had to blow quickly and carefully to spread the glow. I became quite adept at the art of 'fire' making for the purpose of lighting a cigarette.

The winter months were dragging on relentlessly. There was no news of any kind. We were completely isolated. No new people were coming and the guards were not allowed to talk to us. Besides, they were in no better position than we were, because no radio or newspapers were allowed in camp. The idea of completing the sentence in the camp filled one with despair. I had already spent 14 months in various prisons and the prospect of enduring another two years in the camp appeared an impossibility. Anyway, there was good evidence that no one had ever left the camp. When the sentence neared completion the authorities found a reason for extending the stay.

This was called 'dobavka', an addition, in most cases for some imaginary offence committed, or simply, because of some administrative mix-up. Some people let themselves be overcome with depression and hopelessness and were visibly changing into shadows of themselves; others kept on fighting in an unexplained and unjustified belief that the time would come when freedom would dawn again. Our 'Diesiatnik', the koolak with a 10 year sentence to serve, often repeated his philosophy: 'if you want to live try to work hard to get your bread ration and eat every crumb of it'. 'They won't last for ever', he would add prophetically. I subscribed to this philosophy, though at times I was so exhausted and depressed that I wished for a speedy end to existence.

THE TOOL SHED

Suddenly and for no reason known to me I was taken out from the snow clearing and stump uprooting team and assigned to the tool making shed. That was a most welcome change of fortune. In the tool making shed there worked three people: an elderly carpenter cum smith, his assistant, a 'do it yourself' all-rounder and an 18 year old, tall, bright, cheerful Ukrainian, named Vasil. I was sent there as a general helper. The shed was a small wooden structure, one part of which was used as a store of raw material, that is, logs of wood, axes and saws; the larger, centre part was used as a working place and a repository of finished tools. In one of the corners was a stove which was kept going continuously by feeding in scraps of wood and shovel-fulls of sawdust. A warm and cosy place. An oasis in the ocean of misery.

Here there were no 'provierkas', those dreadful evening roll calls, and though sleeping conditions weren't any better than in the barrack, one had a feeling of privacy. We were not supervised but we had to work hard to make sure that there were enough axes and saws in good order for everybody the following morning. That meant a great deal of honing and filing, replacing handles of axes and shovels and making new ones. A few hundred people had to be supplied with tools and that was our responsibility. We worked overnight and we rested during the day. The master carpenter was not given to talking and usually got on with his work quietly. He kept a friendly eye on the rest of us. His assistant, Alex, liked to enter into political discussions, and in spite of his imprisonment, he remained a convinced communist and supporter of the Soviet Union.

When challenged with the question whether it was right for the Soviet Union to sign a pact of friendship and co-operation with a fascist country like Nazi Germany, his answer was that this was done to enable Germany to fight and destroy the capitalist countries, Britain and France, and when as a result of the war Germany would get exhausted, the Soviet Union would step in and extend its socialist order over the whole of Europe. A neat solution. As I found out later, this view was held by many and no doubt, was prompted by years of anti-capitalist propaganda.

The young Ukrainian, Vasil, hardly ever spoke but instead would hum Ukrainian tunes and at times, sing a song. His exclusive job was making handles for axes. He would choose a log, cut it into several lengths of the required size, place one vertically and with a few blows of an axe would cut away chunks of wood all round a nearly perfect handle. All that was then required to be done to this raw handle was to shape it slightly at the end for a better grip and to plane it smooth. This he did with lightning speed, and the finished product would join the dozen or so others on the bench. Vasil seemed to be in love with the wood he cut and shaped and the material yielded to him as if returning his great affection. A Leonardo da Vinci of the axe handle.

Our food was the usual camp ration, but, at least on one occasion there was a change. One of the four horses that were used for hauling logs, broke a leg and had to be destroyed. Who shot the animal and what happened to the carcass I did not know, but one night a chunk of horse meat appeared in the hut. It had bits of frozen snow on it indicating the way it was kept hidden. That night and subsequent nights there were feasts in our hut. Incidentally, the inmate who worked with that horse was arrested for negligence and no doubt, given a few extra years.

My job was helping with cutting the logs, grinding and touching up axes, clearing away wood chips etc., a general factotum but I liked it, for it provided me with a degree of freedom that many would have wished to have in the prevailing conditions. At dawn we had to be ready to hand out tools to the teams leaving for the forest. First came the 'Stachanovites', an all Russian team whose members claimed to be the best workers and who were very particular about the quality of tools. Then followed the other teams. The procedure went on quietly in the darkness pierced by a solitary paraffin lamp, and only the shout of the guard: 'Shag iv pravo, shag iv levo...' the ritual caution could be heard. When all teams departed there was an eerie silence in the camp and the darkness of the night persisted for some hours yet.

While going about my work in the shed in somewhat more relaxed conditions than previously, I reflected on the fact that though there were many young people like myself in the camp I had never heard a conversation or remark about sex or for that matter, about women. This reminded me of what the woman doctor from the Transit Camp said to me when I asked her what the 'Corrective lager' to which we were being taken, was like. How right she was! No one had any sexual urge, no one ever uttered anything of an erotic nature. We were all automatons: getting up, going to work, dragging our feet back to camp, gulping down the soup and lying down to sleep. It required an unusual effort to muster strength to have any kind of social intercourse.

The regime, though strictly regulated, had no elements of deliberate persecution. There was no beating or excessive harshness, just a policy of getting out maximum work from those strong enough to be able to survive under the extreme camp conditions. There seemed to be a tacit intention to let the weak go to the wall. A cynical policy of cheap labour and exploitation.

WATCHMAN

My work in the tool shed came suddenly to an end. I do not know why; I was never told. It lasted for over two months and enabled me to survive a substantial part of the dreadful Arctic winter in comparative comfort. One morning I was told by my 'Brigadier' that I would be given the job of night watchman. I was to walk out on my own into the forest at the time when the working teams were returning to camp and guard the timber stacks produced during the day. Normally these were taken away by horse and cart to a depot, but very often some were left behind a day or two. Theft of timber must have occurred since the authorities decided that is was necessary to guard it. How and when such theft would take place in the wilderness and remoteness of our camp I could not imagine. Rumours circulated in the camp that the possible thieves were the Russian recidivists who, whenever an opportunity arose, helped themselves to timber from the stacks to build up their own in order to exceed their quota.

At first I had a strange feeling: a mixture of anxiety and excitement. To be in the forest alone all through the night frightened me a lot but the prospect of being my own master for a number of hours filled me with joyous excitement. The first thing I did when I reached the place in the forest was to make a bonfire. This was very necessary in order to keep wolves and beasts at a respectable distance, and of course, to keep warm. It was the beginning of June. The snow had gone only a week or two before and the ground was already covered with patches of grass from which little white flowers courageously rose their heads. Vast sheets of water glimmered in the low hanging Arctic sun. The forest was shedding its winter clothes and getting friendlier with fresh greenness.

Daylight was stretching into the night hours and it only got dark well past midnight. Normally, except for the two and half months of summer, the inmates were leaving for work and returning to camp in pitch darkness. In summer it was still light when the workers returned from the forest and it was then when I used to make my way into the forest.

On the way I would sometimes meet the team in which my friend Michail was and then he would ask me what was for dinner that night and I would inform him that for hors d'oeuvres caviar and for the main course steak and French potatoes followed by etc, etc. He knew perfectly well what to expect.

The guards in our camp were quite young, probably doing their normal military service, but for some reason, possibly as punishment for some misdemeanour, had been sent to take on duties in the far North. A few of them were friendly souls, and though officially they were not allowed to fraternise with prisoners, occasionally one could break the ice and have a few words with them. I managed to get on friendly terms with one of them and asked him to lend me something to read. Until my assignment as watchman I had no opportunity or strength for reading but now conditions were much better, for I had a secure 2nd 'pot' and reasonable rest during the day while the barrack was nearly empty, consequently I felt a strong desire to read something, anything. My friendly guard was sympathetic to my request, but all he could lend me were booklets of short stories about heroic Soviet airmen and patriotic, highly efficient workers - 'Stakhanovites', that is those who not only fulfilled their quotas in the Donbas coal mines but exceeded them twice over.

I wasn't thrilled with this choice of literature but I gratefully accepted the offer. I used to take these booklets with me into the forest and read them sitting by the bonfire. There was sufficient light for reading well into the late hours of the night. I wasn't impressed by the 'heroic' achievements of the Soviet airmen and I was sorry for the miners who were slogging their guts out for a pittance and the 'glory' of being included in the ranks of heroes of the Soviet Union.

Alone in the forest I experienced the first time for over 19 months the beauty of nature. Trees which were hitherto objects stubbornly resisting the axe and saw of the feller transformed into friendly, living creatures, gently swaying in the breeze. The moss and lichen were in places sprinkled with little wild flowers whose names I didn't know; there was an abundance of young trees, mere striplings with fresh leaves and tender, skin-thin bark - all this was like a revelation. I thought fleetingly of home, of my little town, the stream that ran not far from my house and in which I used to paddle when I was a child. But that was a long time ago. I had no illusions about life in invaded Poland. I had dreadful premonitions and the impossibility of getting any news from home depressed me greatly.

NAZI GERMANY ATTACKS THE SOVIET UNION

Towards the end of June 1941 something extraordinary happened in the camp. One day a large board appeared on the kitchen wall and on it were pinned front pages of the two major national newspapers 'Pravda' and 'Izviestie' saying the German fascists had attacked our fatherland and the heroic forces of the Soviet Union have stopped the aggressor. But we must be vigilant, for the enemy could try to infiltrate our ranks. The paper showed pictures of enemy aircraft and asked everybody to report the sight of any of those in the sky over the country. Alongside these newspaper pages there was an appeal from the Camp Commander to work harder, to produce more for the country, for our fatherland. A most misguided, cynical and audacious appeal. Some of the Russian inmates could hardly conceal their delight - such was their hatred of the government. A number of long-sentence prisoners volunteered to go to the army, hoping to gain freedom that way. This however did not work.

The Jewish prisoners had mixed feelings. Some of us, being in complete ignorance of what was happening in the German occupied territories, hoped that the attack on the country would prompt the Soviet Government to open the forced labour camps and release the people in order to direct able-bodied men to the Forces, and the rest to work for the war effort, no longer as prisoners but as free human beings. Rays of hope appeared on the horizon, however, many weeks passed without any change in the camp routine. The long hours and the back breaking, exhausting work persisted as before, consequently the simmering hatred of the system did not abate.

There were no papers, no radio only rumours based on bits of information passed on from man to man and originating from a friendly guard. Yesterday's capitalist blood suckers and working class oppressors: the English, the Americans, the French, doomed to vanish from the face of the earth by the hands of the friendly German people, became overnight close friends and comrades-in-arms, and the Germans - a common enemy.

In the Soviet political and social climate such changes were not unusual. The propaganda machine was immediately set in motion and the new political philosophy rammed down your throat. No questions were asked - answers were usually given before even a question had time to germinate in one's head.

SUPERVISOR OF 'BEZPRIZORNIKH' (JUVENILE DELINQUENTS)

Our camp, as almost every other in the Soviet Union had a number of juveniles who were under the same rigours as adult prisoners except that they were assigned to somewhat lighter work. After some weeks as a watchman I was appointed supervisor of a juvenile team. This was promotion but I soon came to regret my acceptance of this post, for nothing had changed in my conditions. I did not get a pair of felt boots, the kind team leaders were entitled to - the envy of everybody in the camp - neither did they put me in a more comfortable barrack together with the privileged leaders. My situation actually worsened.

The team consisted of ten boys, from about ten to sixteen years of age. They had never had a normal family life and not one of them had been at school longer than a few months and at that with breaks for truancy. They were here for pickpocketing, participating in robbery together with adults and persistent begging.

Our job was to tidy up after a tree had been felled and the branches cut off. This involved gathering the branches onto one place, cutting them up into manageable pieces and burning the pieces. The older boys were meant to do the cutting, the younger - collecting the pieces and burning. They all had a natural reluctance to do any work at all, with which I inwardly sympathised, but my responsibility was to see to it that the quota for the day was completed.

The established regulations applied equally to young and old, and reduced bread rations were given to those who did not pull their weight. Most of the boys in my team would rather warm themselves at the fire than do the assigned work, and no amount of cajoling had any effect. They were foul-mouthed and swore after every few words. When I repeated to them the words of wisdom that my supervisor, Strelok, used to utter: 'if you want to survive work for your bread ration' - they would swear at me: 'yob tvoyoo mat'h (fuck your mother) - we managed to live until now without doing any work and we, blast it, intend to go on like that'. In fact, this was true. They seemed somehow to find food, and in spite of reduced rations, contrived to thrive and be quite cheerful.

I was faced with a dreadful dilemma: to denounce the slackers or to resign the 'post' and go back to the old stump digging team.

I tried to reason with the older boys and get them to influence the rest of the team, which worked for a while but the habit of doing as little as possible reasserted itself very quickly. After a fortnight or so I asked to be released from that 'elevated' position and returned to my old team.

The war in the Soviet Union had been on for some weeks and large areas of the country must have been by then invaded by the Nazis. However, we knew virtually nothing about these events, and the camp went on functioning as before. If anything, the quality of bread deteriorated and the soup became thinner. More people than before suffered from scurvy, with the inevitable consequence of falling out of teeth and swelling of limbs. The initial excitement generated by the news of the war subsided and the daily routine returned with all its drabness.

THE AMNESTY

If the prophet Isaiah had turned up one day in the camp and told us that most of the prisoners would soon be set free, he would have been looked upon as being mad. The news came like a bolt from the sky. Polish subjects were to be released in order to form Polish Army units to fight the Germans alongside our 'friends and allies', the units of the glorious Soviet Army. We weren't told any details. We weren't interested in details about the future. All we wanted was to leave the camp and to be free.

It was September 1941. The temperature had been dropping daily and thin snow was already on the ground. Those to be freed were notified and gathered into a separate barrack, but no information was given as to when there would be a transport or where we would be taken. There had been a few Polish subjects whose names had not appeared on the amnesty list and those were naturally tortured by anxiety. The omissions were often a result of administrative inadequacies which were in time corrected, but in the meantime dreadful damage had been done to the morale of some people.

We were now among ourselves, that is, there were no Russian prisoners living in our barrack, but they were allowed to come in and some of them did with the sole intention to steal whenever an opportunity arose. Few of us had much of value, but some managed to retain one or two vests or perhaps a shirt or a pair of socks. These were treasures that had to be closely guarded, but just the same, theft occurred. Often one knew exactly who came into the barrack and helped himself to the missing object, but nothing could be done to retrieve the thing. If approached the thief would not deny the theft, he would smile cynically and say: 'You are going out, you don't need these rubbishy pieces of clothes, you will be able to get much better things. We are here for good. This is our life'. There was no answer to that and it would have been futile to report the theft. It had been tried before but the authorities had never made any effort to recover stolen goods. The result of being deprived of any of the most essential pieces of clothing meant misery from cold and often fatalities caused by frost-bite and hypothermia.

A few days later we were taken by lorries to the nearest railway stations about 50 miles away, and put into a passenger train. The Commander of the transport was a Russian officer, and although there were no armed guards, the fact that a Russian was in charge, made us all suspicious. We did not feel free and we behaved timidly. No official announcement was made as to the destination of the transport, but rumours spread that the train was going to Kirov. We travelled two days with long stops at various places, but we were told not to distance ourselves from the train because there would be no other train going that way. We were given the usual camp bread ration, but at least there was an adequate supply of water.

At Kirov the Russian Commandant handed over his duties to the Polish authorities. This was, we felt, a moment of historical significance. We were told that Polish Forces would be formed somewhere in the South and we would be travelling there to join some already existing units. Where exactly the place was and how long the journey would take no one seemed to know.

The train rolled along towards Kazan, where we stopped for quite a few weeks. Most of us lived in tents in conditions not much different from those in camp. Winter was closing in and the only way to keep warm was to stand close to a bonfire of which there were several spread over the area, and in the early evening, to retire to the tent, tuck in as best one could under the only blanket that each one had been given.

However, the discomfort did not matter much and hardly anybody complained. There was a tremendous feeling of joyful expectation, a longing for the wheels of history to turn faster and events to unfold. A sort of feeling one had when on the 3rd of September 1939 Great Britain declared war on Germany. Now that Britain, America and the Soviet Union were fighting the Nazis, it wouldn't take long to bring the war to a victorious end.

At that stage we knew very little what was happening on the war fronts and absolutely nothing about life at home, that is in Poland, under occupation.

I thought about my family quite often, but I could never

have imagined the conditions under which they had to live. I often reproached myself for having run away from home. I felt selfish, but thought at times, perhaps conditions, though hard under occupation, would allow them to survive the war which, no doubt would now, with the help of the Soviet Union, not last very long.

One evening standing at the bonfire I felt suddenly very hot and started shivering. A few moments later I fainted. When I came round in the hospital, I was told that I had pneumonia and would have to stay in bed until the temperature dropped. It was the first time for nearly two years that I slept in a bed with clean sheets and a pillow. I was too exhausted and feverish to fully enjoy it, but just the same, I appreciated the change. The temperature dropped much too soon and after about ten days, I was ordered to leave the hospital and go back to the tent.

The camp was expanding rapidly; more tents were being put up, and the few wooden buildings in the centre were bursting at the seams. The monotony of waiting was interrupted by funerals of people who had been in the hospital for only a few days and had died of typhoid or other illnesses caused by malnutrition or infections. The sombre processions following a black cloth covered coffin became almost a daily routine. One hardened to that sight. It was only a matter of numbers. The danger of an epidemic was imminent and tremendous efforts were made under the most arduous conditions: austerity and shortage of most elementary medicines, to contain the disaster.

In the mean time a large number of people succumbed and died.

It must have been more than six weeks later when we were told that a train would be available to take us further south. Soon we were heading for Kuybishev where the Headquarters of the forming Polish Forces was situated.

Some resemblance of organisation was in evidence. After more formal registration of personal details based on no more than information provided by the person being registered, since no written documents were available, we were divided into Companies and Squads and commanders of these units were appointed. The commanders were former officers and Non-Commissioned officers. Though still in tents with subzero temperatures, conditions were better than before and were steadily improving.

GUZAR

This small village near Kuybishev, ASSR, was now our Army camp. We were free, at least within the confines of the camp. We spoke Polish and we hoped that one day in the near future we would be able to leave the Soviet Union. Living under canvas in winter months when the temperature dropped at times to minus 20 was hard, but we bore the hardship cheerfully. The overwhelming consideration was to keep reasonably warm and to recover normal strength. We had no uniforms, but gradually, though at unpredictable times, some pieces of warm clothing would be made available and so, after some weeks, we managed to be clothed adequately to withstand the rigours of the winter. We had no arms and there was no regular army training. There were however daily physical exercises to improve our fitness, but the main occupations for most of us were going out in teams into the neighbouring forest to collect twigs for our camp fires, the only source of heat, and peeling potatoes, virtually the only food available to us.

The initially amorphous crowd began to take the shape of a normal military organisation. The smallest unit, the squad, was usually housed in one tent. Three squads formed a platoon and three platoons a company, in charge of which was an officer, usually a lieutenant. In spite of the boring routine, a spirit of hope and expectation pervaded the people. We knew very little about the current fortunes of the war since there was no radio and no papers, but just the same morale was excellent.

At some later time I was delegated by my Company Commander to go every day at 3 o'clock in the afternoon, to Headquarters in order to take notes of a daily Bulletin read to us by the Battalion Education Officer. In fact, every Company had its representative, a kind of information officer, to collect news from H.Q. Armed with these notes of the latest events, each delegate, usually somebody with secondary school education, would read the information taken at H.Q. in front of his Company when it assembled for the evening tattoo.

It was a somewhat privileged position and it gave me satisfaction that I was first in my Company to know what was going on.

The news was very limited and usually, as found out later, heavily biased towards presenting successes of the Soviet Army and omitting defeat. The truth was that from the beginning of the invasion of the Soviet Union in June 1941 the German forces were moving very fast through the Western territories of Russia and the Ukraine and only later in 1942 they were at some points halted for some time. We had no idea what was happening to the civilian population in the Nazi-conquered countries.

Thoughts about my family were continuously recurring but there was no way of getting any concrete news. It was impossible to know what could have happened to the people at home, to the Jewish population in particular, and the absence of any clue made it difficult to imagine what their situation might be. The result was a blank, a void, a feeling of helplessness.

Since the Polish Army in the Soviet Union was formed from the inmates of Forced Labour Camps, the composition of the Units was very unconventional. Firstly, the ages within a unit varied from as young as 17 to over 40 and the standard of education from secondary illiteracy to academic.

In the first stages of formation of the Polish Forces most able-bodied Polish subjects were enlisted (why not all is explained later), consequently there was a large proportion of retired officers in the budding army. The war against the invading German army in Poland lasted a few days only and most of the serving officers were taken prisoner. Similarly, when the Soviet Army invaded the Eastern part of Poland on the 17th September 1939, the Polish Forces were disarmed and the officers taken prisoner. A large number of these prisoner-officers was incarcerated in Katyn and shot. The Soviet authorities asserted that the crime had been committed by the Nazis, but recently convincing evidence was produced that the Polish officers from Katyn were shot by the K.G.B. - the Soviet secret police. As a result the newly formed Polish units had very few young officers and a surplus of older Captains, Majors and Non-Commissioned officers. Since rightly or wrongly ranks were honoured, we found ourselves with a large number of officers, at least in the early stages. One easily accepts the sight of a grey haired general or colonel, but a sub-lieutenant or lieutenant or even captain who is burdened with age and blessed with baldness or greyness and a stooping figure, does not exactly inspire admiration or respect. It was at times quite amusing to watch scene of these elderly low ranking officers trying to cut a figure, straining themselves to marching stiffly, and if put in charge of a company, to be over strict. One of these, as it happened an intellectual, was for some time a Company Commander. Despite considerable efforts to be very 'military' he did not succeed to convince the colonel that he was suitable for the job, consequently he was moved, to his great chagrin, from the 'front' line to another, on the face of it, very important position.

We were an Army but, as mentioned before, without arms and without the knowledge of how to use them. There were among us, some Non-Commissioned officers but their knowledge of warfare was limited and outdated. There was a need for up-to-date instructions, for acquaintance with modern weaponry and methods. We were still in the Soviet Union and had no access to Western sources, and of necessity had to fall back on Russian military literature. That was when our unsuccessful intellectual lieutenant came into the picture. He knew Russian well and he was asked to translate a Russian army instruction manual.

Since there were no copying facilities, each company sent out one man to H.Q. where the work was being done, to write down the translated text for subsequent use within the

Company. At H.Q. in one of the larger rooms tables were assembled in the letter 'U' form, the officer would sit at the top table and would read the Russian text, translate it into Polish and the scribes would write down the translation. I was one of those scribes, probably because I had a smattering of Russian and occasionally could suggest a correct Polish word for a Russian expression.

This work went on for several weeks. I considered myself lucky to have this job, for the routine of the camp was extremely boring. One event broke the monotony. One freezing morning we were told that the Soviet Foreign Minister Vyshinsky would visit us in a couple of days and we would have to parade in front of him.

We were now 'comrades in arms' dedicated to fight the common enemy, however no arms were yet available and training was limited to some physical exercises and some rudimentary knowledge of topography in relation to infantry combat. The main occupation was still collecting wood from the neighbouring forest to keep warm.

The visit by the Soviet Foreign Minister was obviously going to be an important event and some intensive rehearsing of the forthcoming parade was the order of the day. The great day eventually came. It was a crisp frosty morning. We had by then some kind of uniforms, an assortment that could be described as being a hybrid between civic and military: similar trousers but differing jackets and differing boots, but somehow the commanders of respective units managed to assort their troops such as to achieve a degree of uniformity. So far so good, but how could we face a frost of minus twenty degrees with bare hands, for gloves were the item of clothing sadly missing from our outfit?

The clever solution to the problem came from the Stores Officer who suggested to wear identical socks in place of gloves. The parade was a great success. Comrade Vyshinsky, a distinguished and kind-faced looking gentleman smiled, visibly satisfied with the event. Was he the same man who, as the chief prosecutor, demanded the death sentence for Zinoviev, Kamieniev, Radek and other communist leaders at the infamous 1937 trials?!

EXODUS FROM THE SOVIET UNION

The day one longed and waited for, and hardly believed that it would ever come, had actually arrived. Unexpected orders and sudden changes are not unusual in the army. This was particularly true during the war and in the normally prevailing atmosphere of secrecy in the Soviet Union. Nothing was said until the day before it happened and no more was revealed in the Order than that we were to take all our belongings and be ready the following morning for a journey by lorries to an undisclosed destination.

In fact the destination was Krasnovodsk, a port at the Caspian Sea. There, in the port were already tied up several large open ferries. We were divided into groups and ordered to embark. On some of the ferries there were already groups of civilians: men, women and children, who, as we discovered later, were Polish families who were also set free from what was called 'volnaya zsilkal', an expression meaning literally 'free exile', a contradiction in terms if ever there was one. Actually, it was a compulsory punishment of thousands of people, whole families, to remote places in the Asian part of the Soviet Union where they were allocated to various tasks in villages or collectives. They were not allowed to leave the area but were not under guard. Conditions they lived in were very severe indeed: crammed accommodation and hard work.

On embarkation we were greeted emotionally by those

civilian families. There was an unusual air of urgency to get on the ferry and to get away as speedily as possible, and indeed, as soon as the ferry was full, it pulled away from the shore.

Suddenly somebody in the middle of the ferry started singing a well known religious hymn and immediately the whole crowd picked it up, and an intense sound of tearful joy rose into the air. Some knelt and prayed, some cried. A feeling of incipient freedom pervaded, not yet complete freedom, for we were still on a Russian vessel in Russian waters. One wanted to shout, to give vent to the suppressed longing for normal life, but uncertainties lingered and stifled the emotion. The feeling of a momentous turn of fortune was general.

After several hours sailing we arrived at Bandar Shah, a small port in Iran, situated at the South Eastern corner of the Caspian Sea. It was early afternoon in March 1942 when we landed on Persian soil. It was also for the first time for two and a half years that I saw stalls with fruit and vegetables and vendors waiting to serve people. We had no money and we looked at the goods with strong desire, hungry for the oranges, figs, nuts. Some could not control their passion and managed to barter away an item of their underwear for food. Some could not control their appetite and became ill from overeating.

We were now Polish Forces under British command and the Western influence became rapidly stronger. British uniforms, boots and the usual military equipment were provided, and

Polish insignia (white eagle, division etc.) were added to mark national identity. After a few days at Bandar Shah we moved to a place near Teheran where a reorganisation into battalions, companies, platoons and teams took place. The general standard of health improved thanks to normal food and exercise and regular military training began. Communication with people from various units helped to partially fill in the gaps in knowledge of events that took place after my detention, but very little was known about what happened in Poland in the previous two years. We knew that the Germans were encountering stiff resistance from the Soviet Forces, but one could read between the lines of communiqués that they were still very successful in their march into the depth of Russia. An occurrence that disturbed me greatly and caused even anxiety was that the Polish authorities, while registering Polish subjects who were released from the various forced labour camps, discriminated against Jews. There was a tendency not to accept Jews into the army which was being formed, but, since this could not have been done legally, all sorts of subterfuges and imaginary reasons were used. As a result of that action, which presumably must have been complying with a directive from higher authorities, separate Jewish Units were formed.

Although of significance and reminiscent of anti-Semitic events in pre-war Poland, this policy was not general and a number of Jews could be found in various units of the Polish Forces. It is perhaps appropriate at this point to mention what happened to my friend who, after having been released from a camp and transported together with hundreds of others to the Kuybishev area, presented himself to the Polish Recruiting Officer. His name was Adam Wohlfeiler; he was a student, well spoken, tall and of good physique. The officer hesitated and after some thought, suggested to him to put down under the item Religion: "Roman Catholic" implying that an easy passage would thus be secured. Adam emphatically declined the 'offer' and the officer grudgingly put him on the list.

After a short stay in the port we travelled in army lorries to the vicinity of Teheran where we were accommodated in huge factory buildings which had been a year or so previously erected by the German industrialist Krupp in anticipation of the invasion of the Middle East by the 'victorious' wehrmacht. Krupp intended to manufacture arms and munitions using cheap Persian labour or, more likely, slave labour, as was the case in Germany at that time.

Garrison life unavoidably imposed restrictions of movement and a measure of discipline but the feeling of no longer being constantly under guard, the feeling of participating, in however modest a capacity, in the fight against the evils of Nazism was a tremendous boost to one's morale.

TOBRUK AND EL-ALAMEIN

The war in the African Desert is the subject of numerous books and here I will only mention that Polish units were actively engaged in the various battles, particularly in the battle of Tobruk. These units formed the Carpathian Regiment which, after the defeat of Rommel's Army by British Forces under the command of Montgomery at El-Alamein, was moved to the Middle East, reorganised and trained in preparation for action in Europe. Some of our units, that is, those formed in the Soviet Union, were incorporated into the Carpathian Division, which had absorbed the Carpathian Regiment. The rest became a part of the newly formed 5th Division, the somewhat frivolously and gently derisively called 'Russian Orthodox' division, since almost everybody serving in it came from the Eastern part of Poland which had been incorporated into the Soviet Union at the beginning of the war.

The few months stay in the garrison near Teheran were marked by training and the usual army routine. There was a small number of Jewish soldiers in my battalion and with the approaching Jewish New Year, Rosh Hashana, and then Yom Kippur, we were invited by the Teheran Jewish Community to come to the Synagogue. The Synagogue, though not impressive from outside, was very beautiful inside. It was oriental and colourful and so very different from those I knew in Poland. After the service there was a Kiddush (blessing of wine and reception) and plenty of food. We were entertained lavishly. It was however difficult to communicate since none of us could speak Persian and only some of the hosts knew a little Russian. This did not prevent us having a very pleasant time in that most congenial atmosphere.

In early summer 1943 we were transferred to an Army camp near Ahuas, one of the hottest spots in Iran. We lived in tents and trained in the surrounding desert and hills at the edge of the Bakhtiar Mountains.

I got to know almost everybody in my Company but I could not find anybody of similar background and common interests. Luckily in the neighbouring Company there were two chaps, both Jewish and from Cracow with whom I found a common language. Jurek, the older of the two, had studied law at Cracow University at the same time as I studied Chemistry there and his and my political views were much the same. We were both socialists and it was surprising that we hadn't met in Cracow, since we both attended the same public meetings, knew the leaders of the students socialists group ZNMS, shared similar taste in literature and art. David was a very pleasant young man, cheerful and much under Jurek's influence.

The three of us used to meet and talk, and if possible, spend leaves together. One particular conversation with Jurek remained vividly in my mind. My erstwhile sympathy for the Soviet Union had been mercilessly crushed by the cruel reality of the system. When still at school, in the early thirties, I was inclined towards communist views, though I had never been a member of the Communist Party. The trials of the communist leaders in 1937 shook my confidence in the integrity of the Soviet Judiciary and the Communist Party and ever since I viewed political events in the Soviet Union with suspicion.

However, the fact that the Soviet Union was perhaps the only country in the world denouncing fascism and nazism and officially forbidding any anti-Semitism activities, kept my loyalty, though without warmth. My friend Jurek found it very difficult to change his views, and in spite of the Friendship Pact between the Soviet Union and Nazi Germany signed in 1939 which resulted in the carving up of Poland by the two 'friendly' nations, and in spite of the existence of the hated Soviet forced labour camps, he could not help himself defending Stalin's rule. He believed that there must have been good reason for doing away with the early Communist leaders. Our disagreement on this point did not however affect our close friendship which has been alive for many years.

TRANSPORT TO PALESTINE

Movement of Forces during the war was wrapped in secrecy and no one apart from the highest authorities knew where our next destination would be. We embarked at Bandar Shahpur and travelled southwards in the Persian Gulf. Apart from some guard duty and keeping the ship clean, there was little to occupy one's time and so I started to study English.

There were no Polish-English textbooks in the ship's library, but I found a German-English textbook. Though somewhat too advanced for a beginner, I managed to make use of it, and acquired some smattering of the language. The journey was pleasant, the palm trees along the banks of the Gulf, the beautiful sunsets and the glistening water in the strong sunshine delighted the eye. We passed through the Straits of Hormuz, rounded the Peninsula and after some days arrived in Aden, where we were told, we would stay for some time. It transpired that our ship had broken down and we were to wait for another ship to continue our journey. It was July, probably the hottest month of the year at one of the hottest places of the Saudi-Arabian peninsula. Our activities there consisted of exercising in the early morning, from 6am to 9am, and sport in the late afternoon. There was a ban on staying outside the tent from 11am to 3pm, an enforced protective measure to avoid sun stroke.

In Aden there were also a RAF unit and some other

auxiliary British military units. One of the sports events that clings to my memory was a football match between our team and an RAF team. We were out in force and so were the British, officers and other rank, and the respective Commanders - both colonels in rank. The two teams, each standing smartly in a row, were facing each other. The two colonels, each having welcomed the opposing team, sat down next to each other, and the match began. There was a lot of cheering and prompting by supporters of respective sides, but all in good spirit and with exemplary behaviour. A truly friendly competition. We still had an exaggerated notion of English gentlemenliness and our boys controlled their enthusiasm so as not to be accused of lack of culture. The match had its drama, but it ended with two all, so no exuberance or depression on either side were registered.

As to be expected in conditions of army life, the problem of sex played an important part, particularly after years of sex starvation. As usual, especially so in the poorer countries of the Middle-East, the solution was provided by commercial sex. There were many brothels in Aden and although the red light district was out of bounds, the chaps found their way to the various establishments to find gratification. The Arabs we had contact with were camp cleaners, some working on buildings and roads, all very humble and addressing the British as Sahib.

There was a Jewish community in Aden and during the High Holydays of Rosh Hashana and Yom Kippur, Jewish soldiers were given leave to go to the local Synagogue. There were about half a dozen of us. When we arrived at the Synagogue we were greeted most cordially, were given fezes to put on, and after the service, which was of the Sephardi style, there was a Kiddush and a modest reception. The vast majority of the community were manual workers, scraping a living by menial tasks.

Jews in Aden were underprivileged and had no access to higher education nor did they have the means of gaining qualifications for other than simple employment. I managed to communicate with some in Hebrew. The traditional prayer: 'Next year in Jerusalem' was a crie de coeur, most sincerely uttered by these people.

After about 6 weeks stay in Aden we continued our journey northwards in the Red Sea. Again, no information was given to the rank and file about our destination. Our next stay was at Ismaila, a small Arab village, not far from Port Said, where there was a British Army camp. The few Egyptians we had an opportunity to meet were workers employed in the camp and their wives or daughters who did our washing for us - all rather servile, some to the point of obsequiousness.

NORTH AFRICA AND THE SOVIET UNION

The war in these two continents was reaching a turning point. After the overwhelming successes of the German Forces in the early years of the conflict, the Allies started gaining ground and the fortunes of the war began to change. On the 23rd October 1942 the British 8th Army attacked Rommel's Forces at El-Alamein and in the early days of November, more British and some US units landed in North Africa. The fierce battles and the reversals in the North African Campaign have been well documented, and here only salient points will be mentioned.

On the 23rd January 1943 the 8th Army captured Tripoli and on the 12th May the last German troops in North Africa surrendered.

The war in the Soviet Union, which started with the German attack on the 22nd June 1941 and brought tremendous successes to the German Forces for over 13 months, allowing the Germans to penetrate into the depths of Russia and the Ukraine, had been halted temporarily when on the 2nd February 1943 German troops at Stalingrad surrendered to the Soviet Forces.

The pressure to open a Second Front in Europe was growing and the air raids on German strategic objects on the Continent intensified. On the 16th of May 1943 RAF 'Dam Busters' carried out a most daring and successful, though very costly in casualties, raid, which quite deservedly has been thoroughly analysed, extensively described and made into a very interesting film.

WE CONTINUE OUR JOURNEY TO PALESTINE

We embarked at Port Said, and though not being told where we were going, it soon became known that we were heading for Haifa. This destination had a particular significance for me. I felt a strong emotion, not only because the country we were going to had been the dream and hope of a multitude of Jews, but also because my elder brother, Joshua with his wife, Irene and their only son, Shimshon, lived there.

Joshua was the second eldest of five brothers of whom I was the youngest, and whom I met only once when I was about 10 years old. He, together with the eldest brother, Eliezer, had left home when I was four for Vienna, and naturally, I had no memories of them. Soon after the Nazis occupied Austria, the Jewish population of that country was rounded up and taken to concentration camps. After the annexation of Czechoslovakia, Eliezer, among thousands of others was taken to Theresienstadt, that infamous camp which the Germans once or twice opened to inspection by the International Red Cross. Prior to a Red Cross visit the camp authorities would hand out larger than normal food rations, and on one occasion some tins of sardines for display, but strictly forbade the prisoners to open them. After the visit the tins were collected and taken away.

Only very recently I discovered that after two years of starvation, frequent beating and dehumanisation, my brother was in transport to the death camp Auschwitz, where he died, probably in the gas chambers. I knew him only from letters and photographs. How very dry the few details of my brother's martyrdom sound on paper! He was a Talmudic scholar, but he loved also books on secular subjects and he wrote most interesting letters, which my mother used to read over and over again. I loved to listen, though I did not always understand the meaning of some words.

The journey to Haifa was pleasant and uneventful. It was May. We arrived in the early hours of a bright, sunny and comfortably warm morning. Quite a change from the oppressive heat of the Red Sea and Port Said. After disembarkation we mounted lorries (big Dodges) and were driven somewhere to an army camp. On the way to the camp there were numerous 'Pardesim' - orange groves, with trees in full blossom. Close to them the air was saturated with an intoxicating scent which was carried for miles by the gentle breeze. But there were also sand dunes, empty spaces, rocky hills and stony fields. Our Camp was in a stretch of fields called Hill 69, some 40 miles from Tel-Aviv and was similar to army camps in Egypt and elsewhere in the Middle-East: a few wooden one-storey buildings accommodating stores and office staff, the rest of the ground being taken up by tents.

I was very anxious to get leave as quickly as possible in order to go to Tel-Aviv and see my family.

As expected, my meeting with my brother was emotional. It

was the first time for over four years that I had got together with a close relative. Strangely enough, in spite of the difference in age, and the fact that I had not seen this brother since I was 10, a close family feeling developed, probably because we were both thinking of our parents and our brothers and sisters in Poland under the Nazis.

Joshua knew but did not tell me that our father, of blessed memory, had died some time after I left home, possibly in December '39. He was frail and most probably could not face the dreadful conditions in which the Jewish community found itself under the German occupation.

The news about my father's death was given to me by Yankel Dudkievich, who was practically our neighbour in Jedrzejow and who had emigrated to Palestine in the early thirties. My sister-in-law, Irene, and nephew, Shimshon, who was then probably about 14, were good company and tried to make my stay in Tel-Aviv pleasant and enjoyable. Joshua and Irene worked in the chocolate company Elite, had very modest wages, lived in a two bedroom flat, but were contented. Joshua spoke Hebrew with his son, German with his wife and some sort of Polish with me, though I managed to communicate to an extent in German with all three. We had a cousin, Celia, who was married and had a daughter, Rebecca, five years younger than me. My dear brother thought that Rebecca was just right for me and seriously suggested to me to consider marriage. He obviously wanted to have me as near as possible. Irene had a more practical attitude and dropped a hint that there needed to be a more solid foundation for marriage than just affection. How right she was, for I had no qualifications, no profession, was just a simple soldier on leave. My studies of Chemistry at the Cracow University were interrupted at the outbreak of the war and since then, for nearly two years, I had no opportunity to look at a book, apart from that of the 'History of the Communist Party' which was 'graciously' lent me in one of the Soviet prisons.

Since release and recovery from the trauma, there had been army service under conditions far from conducive to studying. Of course, it never occurred to me to think about marriage and I dismissed the idea as being a joke.

Camp life, as expected, was marked out for me. Training, learning to live an ordered life, but also finding friendship and enjoying periodic outings and leave.

Together with three others from my Company I was assigned to a newly organised Officers Cadet School where we were to undergo special training for future officers. The training was intensive. It consisted of lectures, oral and written tests, field work map reading, orientation, marksmanship, etc. There was very little free time. The course which under normal conditions took probably more than a year, had been condensed to 4 months with the inevitably increased concentration of training. We often felt very tired and on such occasions one regretted entering the Officer Cadet School, but no one resigned. There was a tremendous desire for advancement and achievement.

It could be that this feeling was a reaction to the time spent in prison and labour camps. After graduation we were promoted to the rank of Officer Cadet, the insignia of which was a red and white trimming round the shoulder epaulette and one stripe. There was still a long way to become a fully fledged officer and no special treatment or privileges were bestowed on us, but just the same, we had a sense of pride and we conducted ourselves with decorum and even dignity. Was that an unconscious reaction to the not so distant past when one was deprived of the last vestiges of self-respect, when in order to survive some people rummaged in rubbish heaps for bits of fish skin or rotten potatoes? We felt great, and though the war was raging and it was obvious that we would soon receive marching orders, life was pleasant. Our stay in Palestine came suddenly to an end. We were to pack and be ready for transport to Lebanon. No reason was given to the rank and file, just an order, but it later transpired that we were going to train in the Lebanese mountains. Why mountains? Was it just an extension of our martial skills, or perhaps a more specific purpose? One does not ask questions in the army, particularly in times of war. Our Battalion was stationed near a small village in the mountains, and as usual in the Middle East, we lived under canvas, 10 to 12 to a tent. My recollection is of fine weather, clear skies, shimmering sea surface in the distance and an unfriendly mountain range, offering, no doubt, beautiful vistas, but demanding the utmost physical effort to allow one to get to the top.

The training was very tough indeed. When off duty and with a few hours in hand I and my friend, Jurek, would make our way to the village. The main attraction was an Arab family with two beautiful daughters and a son, all English speaking, cultured and very hospitable. The older daughter was a teacher, the younger, Najjla, was at High School and intended to go to University. We used to sit in their garden, drink coffee and have long, pleasant conversations. Neither of us had the courage to take out either of the girls. Anyway, any such suggestion would most certainly have been rebuffed.

Longer leaves I used to spend in Beirut, a sprawling town, a strange combination of ancient and modern, pretentious in the exquisiteness of a few hotels and Western cabarets, but unashamedly displaying the slums and poverty of a large number of its inhabitants.

On one occasion, my friend Jurek and I ventured into the American University campus, and walking along a tree lined alley, we came to a building with its front door wide open. Passing by we looked in and noticed a large number of pictures on the walls of a very big room. Curiosity prevailed over good manners and we entered the room without ringing the bell or knocking. At that moment a lady came in from the adjoining room and with a friendly smile asked if she could be of help.

Totally embarrassed we explained that we were intrigued by the pictures, whereupon she offered to guide us through the 'gallery' and to answer any questions. As she later told us, she was the wife of Prof. Dodge, the President (Vice-Chancellor) of the American University.

I was much impressed by the garden with beautiful cedars, flower beds, lovely alleys, and generally with the tranquillity of the campus, or so it appeared to me, and I secretly wished I could one day continue my studies in that sort of environment.

Our stay in Lebanon came abruptly to an end. We were told that we would be going into action fairly soon. Nothing specific, as usual, but it was not too difficult to guess that the war theatre we were most likely to be engaged in would be Italy.

The action in Italy started with the landing of Allied Forces in Sicily on the 10th July 1943. A fortnight later Mussolini resigned. Strong resistance in Sicily delayed its invasion by British and US troops until the middle of August. On the 3rd of September Allied troops landed on mainland Italy and 5 days later Italy surrendered to the Allies. But the battle for Italy was far from over, for the Germans threw into the Italian front several divisions of their best troops and dug themselves into the Apennines.

The Allies managed to occupy the Southern part of the country and moved up as far as the southernmost part of the Matese mountains, that is, north of Campobasso. The Germans had built two powerful defence lines, the Gustav and the Hitler lines, across the width of the Apennines and employed their elite forces to defend them. There had been several attempts by Allied Forces to dislodge the Germans from their dug-in positions, but with no success. On the 15th February 1944 the Royal Sussex attacked the German positions on Hill 593, of which more will be said later, with disastrous results they lost 12 Officers and 130 other ranks.

Several battalions of Hindus and Maoris went into action some weeks later with equally tragic results. On the 15th of March 1944 a consolidated, major assault on the German lines took place in which New Zealand, Hindu and British Forces, altogether 9 brigades including an armoured division, participated. There was on that occasion a 3½ hour artillery bombardment: over 500 bombers dropped 1100 bombs and it had been reported that 1200 tons of ammunition had been used.

All this effort was to no avail. The cost in casualties was enormous. It brought home very strongly the conviction that a direct attack on the powerfully defended Gustav and Hitler lines was bound to end in failure. And yet, unless these lines were broken there would be no progress and the way to Rome would be barred. It was a matter of both strategic importance and prestige that Rome was liberated. This was the position on the Italian front when the Polish Forces in the Middle East were about to go into action.

LEAVE IN PALESTINE

Before leaving Lebanon those soldiers who asked for leave were usually given it. Most went to what was then Palestine, usually to Tel-Aviv to have a good time. The bright lights of the metropolis with its big hotels, night clubs, beautiful beaches attracted young people. But one of the greatest attractions were the brothels in Jaffa and most 'leavers' paid visits to these establishments in spite of their being out of bounds. Leaves were usually of 10 to 14 days duration. Rumours started circulating that some of the Jewish soldiers had not returned from their leave and in fact a friend of mine, also an officer cadet, appeared to be missing after a leave in Palestine.

These facts created a very unpleasant atmosphere, and as usual, snide remarks about Jews deserting and Jews being disloyal and Jews being cowards etc. abounded. Despite that further leaves were given. When I asked for leave to visit my family in Tel-Aviv my Company Commander smiled sardonically and said 'no doubt you won't come back' and not waiting for my comments, left the office. However, I did get my leave and went to Tel-Aviv.

I had strong feelings about the immorality of desertion. I realised perfectly well the reasons why some Jewish soldiers wished to leave the Polish Forces. Most remembered conditions at home: the rising anti-Semitism, the near official boycott of Jewish shops, the strong sympathetic feeling of the ruling circles to fascism; for Jewish prospective students, there were generally numerus clausus at universities and at some faculties - numerus nullus - all this was enough to make one wish to sever connections with the past, with the country that did not want them and the people who despised them.

No detailed knowledge was available to us at that time about events in Poland but what everybody knew and remembered from the early days of the war was the attitude of most of the population to Jews when the Nazis invaded the country.

They remembered the crowds of peasants and town louts following Gestapo officers who promised to let them loose in Jewish shops, and the delight with which they helped themselves to Jewish property at the encouragement of the Nazis. These memories were strong, and though currently there was little manifestation of anti-Semitism, the shadow of the past was ever present. Some may have thought that there was nothing to go back to, and though there was no information about the tragic events that befell the Jewish population in the invaded countries, they felt intuitively that the destruction of the community was so great that the losses could not be redressed.

Did these thoughts occur to me and did I ever entertain the idea of deserting? No doubt my recollections of life in pre-war Poland were equally clouded with anti-Semitic events. At the grammar school (Gymnazium) I was not discriminated against and relations with at least some of the non-Jewish class mates were quite reasonable, though outside school there was very little common social life. Most of the teachers, again, showed no obvious dislike of the Jewish pupils, but, occasionally, and almost unconsciously, there manifested itself a patronising and sardonic spirit, as if to say, 'your place is really not here and be grateful for being given the privilege'. A sort of polite anti-Semitism.

It would have been surprising if some of the teachers would not have been influenced by the barrage of anti-Jewish propaganda in the right wing press, and that was the press most teachers, who, as the educated elite belonging to the middle class, read.

Later, at the Cracow University, where I studied Chemistry, there was a complete change of the social scenario. Jewish students did not mix with non-Jews. The Polish students corporation 'Bratniak' was an anti-Jewish right wing, extremely nationalistic organisation with strong fascist leanings. Its aim, ostensibly, was the welfare of students but, in fact, its main task was organising the annual blockade against the entry of Jewish students to lecture halls.

This occurred usually at the beginning of the academic year. Pickets were positioned outside lecture halls, some armed with sticks. Police were not allowed to enter the University courts and so some 'Bratniak' members, for whom the name hooligans would be more fitting, were free to cause disruption and chaos.

Jewish students did not take this lying down and it often came to bloody confrontation with casualties on both sides. At times the 'Bratniak' decided that Jewish students would be allowed into lecture halls but they must sit on the left hand side benches, thus creating a sort of ghetto. This, of course, was strongly resisted by us, and again, the conflict often ended in a fight. These events left indelible memories of the 'good' old times.

However, there was a sizeable group of non-Jewish students who belonged to the organisation called ZNMS (independent young socialists), small in numbers compared with the reactionary 'Bratniak', but truly liberal in outlook, progressive, anti-fascist and defending the rights of the oppressed.

I was a member of this organisation and I genuinely believed that our work was useful and eventually our effort would bear fruit. Our Organisation was affiliated to the Polish Socialist Party, which in the twenties was strong and influential, but had been decimated and suppressed in the thirties by the increasingly reactionary government.

All this was 3-4 years before. Now the war was raging and the intention was to defeat the enemy and to free Europe from Nazi slavery. The war was against tyranny, for freedom and justice. I often thought that one could only be certain of the first of this trinity: I knew who we fought against but wasn't sure whether the other two aims would be achieved.

My leave in Tel-Aviv was coming to an end. The several desertions of Jews from the Polish Forces became generally known to the Jewish community and exaggerated tales were circulating about a huge Jewish exodus because of anti-Semitism. I had been at times under inquisitive questioning why I was still wearing a uniform. My late brother would have liked the idea of my staying in Palestine but had never tried to persuade me to leave the Forces. I had never any doubt where my loyalties lay. It wasn't patriotism, the sort of romantic, sugary cake one was fed with at school, it wasn't memories of a particularly happy childhood or youth that kept any loyalties unscathed. Two factors were uppermost in my mind whenever anyone mentioned the possibility of staying behind in Palestine: the oath I had taken and perhaps a chance of finding somebody from my family who might have survived by a miracle. The oath had meant a great deal to me. No doubt I would have been laughed at by many if I confessed to that feeling, therefore I never mentioned it to anyone.

I have never been a strictly religious Jew, that is, I never thought that the various traditional observances are the essence of religion, but I always had a very deep feeling about the ethics of religion. Having been brought up in a very religious home, I used to lay Teffilin every morning and go to Synagogue with my late father. At the University the ritual disappeared, but a religious feeling remained. There were times when atheistic doubts kept invading my mind and I struggled to reach some sort of conclusion, but my efforts were in vain. I could not, and cannot, for instance, reconcile myself with the idea that Jews are the chosen people, not even, as some rabbis assert, they are chosen not for any particular merits or special qualities but for a special mission to mankind.

I could not make myself believe that the Jewish religion is the only true religion, that other monotheistic religions are inferior or false. I could not accept that everything in the Torah, the Old Testament - as the Christians call it, is of divine origin. And yet I have a strong religious sentiment. I would not break an oath and I would be quite unhappy if I forgot to pay up a donation, the promise of which I made at the open scrolls. Is it for fear of retribution? Possibly. A lie does not come easily to me. I feel a strong revulsion about lying, but I do make a distinction between a lie with moral or material consequences and a social fib that does harm to no one and very often smoothes social relations. I am afraid I am guilty of the latter and I feel no pangs of conscience over it.

I think of God a great deal though I do not understand Him. I have a lot of unanswered questions, most are probably unanswerable. Does He intervene in human affairs? Or has He let loose the human race, and having bestowed on its members as much evil as good, allowed them to play out the human drama? If so, God could be accused of a bizarre sense of humour. One cannot black out ones brain and forbid it to search for the truth. It is not satisfactory to say that divine will and divine wisdom are unfathomable, cannot be grasped by a human brain, and leave it at that. It is of course, much easier to leave theology alone and carry on with life as best one can.

This inevitably leads to hypocrisy and moral compromise, which seems to be socially quite acceptable. One does not talk about it; one practices it.

I often wonder whether God wants us to remind Him several times a day how all-powerful He is, how magnificent and compassionate, and to assure Him of our loyalty. I find the phrase 'for I am a jealous God' distasteful and highly uncomplimentary. I do not pray a lot but the thought of God is ever present with me. Is it an inadmitted notion that by thinking of God I shall be spared misfortune? Yet, why should I be so much better off than thousands of others? Why have my mother, two brothers, three sisters, brother-in-law and two nieces been murdered in Nazi concentration camps together with millions of others? It is obviously not a case of wickedness being punished, for among the six million Jews who perished in the Holocaust were hundreds of thousands of innocent children, and thousands of saintly people. Does God care for individuals, or for whole nations? There is no evidence. Does this undermine my faith? At times painful doubts creep into my mind, but soon a strange force brings me back to my faith. This must have been presumably the source of power of my oath.

ITALY - OUR FINAL DESTINATION

From Lebanon we travelled in lorries down South to Port Said where we embarked on ships to sail to Italy.

Though the Mediterranean had already been freed from enemy ships, there was still a real danger from the air and strict precautions had to be taken. Luckily we were spared unpleasant encounters and we landed safely in Taranto, a small port in Southern Italy.

We were reminded of our luck by the Battalion Commander, who must have got to know about complaints of congested conditions on the boat, for a previous transport had been bombed and had suffered heavy casualties.

We quickly disembarked and proceeded by lorries to the vicinity of Matera, a small town north-west of Taranto. We set up camp and lived in small camouflaged tents. Our duties were patrolling and training in this new territory.

The Italian front had been for many months firmly established, the Germans having entrenched themselves in the mountain range close to the monastery of Monte Cassino. After several unsuccessful attempts to dislodge them, the Allied Command must have resolved that only a concerted, well prepared and powerful offensive with elements of surprise and readiness to accept heavy casualties might defeat the enemy. The notion that Italy is a country of sun and song was quickly dispelled, for there was snow on the hills, slush on the ground, a cold wind and grey skies, most of the winter months. Our camp consisted of numerous small tents, housing two or three persons and pitched over a rectangular cavity, about 3 ft deep and 2 ft wide, so as to allow one to stand upright inside the tent. On both sides of the cavity the ground formed benches on which mattresses were placed for sleeping. The tents, being very low and camouflaged, were hardly visible, certainly not from a distance of 100 yards.

I decided to use my spare time, and there were several hours a day when one was off duty, to learn Italian, but no English-Italian text book was available, let alone a Polish-Italian, so I settled for a German-Italian which was bought for me in Bari by a friend who happened to have spent some of his leave there.

I took a liking to the language and progressed reasonably quickly to the stage that I could communicate in short, simple sentences with the contadini (the peasants) in the villages we patrolled, and to utter a few pleasantries to the girls one occasionally encountered. Life was reasonably relaxed and apart from the usual precautions, such as black-out and strict avoidance of larger gatherings, one enjoyed the new environment in spite of uncomfortable living conditions.

Italy has always been associated with wine and the word 'chianti' had been known to everybody, so, no wonder that attempts to procure wine were often made. There were no shops where we were stationed, and anyway, even if there were any, no wine would have been for sale. The only possible sources of wine were with some farmers who might have hidden the stuff, and so our boys went sometimes in search of such a source.

When asked for wine, a farmer would say: 'niente, i tedeschi portano via', (there is none, the Germans have taken it away), but on one occasion some secret information was revealed to the seekers of the beverage. A farmer, who evidently did not like his neighbour, when asked whether he had any wine for sale, said that he has none, but the chap next door had buried a barrel of wine in the middle of his garden under a particular tree. This valuable information was made use of by two lads from our Company.

Both armed themselves with mine detectors, and when the farmer in question denied having wine, they said they wanted to search the garden, then, starting from the gate they went round the garden in ever decreasing circles, covering the whole ground with the detector, until they came to the tree under which the barrel was hidden. There they stopped and thoroughly went over the ground under the tree several times and finally delivered a firm statement: 'Here is wine, a lot of it'. The farmer was stunned. He crossed himself, admitted and asked to be forgiven. Then he said: 'the Germans, the New Zealanders, the French - they all looked here for wine, but they could not find it. You must be extraordinarily clever to have detected it'.

Leave was usually spent in Bari - a large port with over a quarter of a million population. The town offered possibilities of relaxation and amusement, but above all, the availability of signorinas in a number of brothels. One had to be very careful, and it was a punishable offence to frequent a brothel without condoms which were provided free by the doctor's surgery before going on leave. Rumours abounded that the Germans planted syphilitic prostitutes in brothels in Southern Italy to spread the disease among Allied Forces. In spite of strict orders and precautions there were cases among our troops of contagion and a clinic was established to provide cure.

On one of my leaves I witnessed a powerful explosion, luckily from a safe distance. An ammunition ship lying in the harbour blew up hurtling huge chunks of steel, sheet iron and timber a hundred feet into the air. This resulted in numerous casualties and considerable damage to the buildings and installations of the port. Was it sabotage or an accident? It was never discovered.

After this relatively easy and relaxing period near Matera, our Division moved further North to the vicinity of Campobasso, a town very close to Cassino where the German Forces had built their defensive line. As mentioned earlier, the Germans guarded their positions from the Gustav line, which consisted of deep, cut in rock, reinforced bunkers, defended by the best paratrooper and other, experienced in battle, troops.

Here again we lived in small twin, camouflaged tents at the

bottom of the hills, but under a much stricter regime: in addition to a complete blackout and restricted movement, we were not allowed to take off our boots or clothes when lying down to sleep. The whole camp was under continuous guard, day and night.

We patrolled quite close to the enemy line, often between and over mine fields, consequently there were cases of mine explosions and fatal accidents. Those were the first real war experiences that brought home the realisation of one's vulnerability and exposure to mortal danger. Inevitably the atmosphere became sombre and the imminent danger triggered off in some of us a sort of nervous cynicism.

One of my patrols is worth recalling, not for its exploits or particular danger from the enemy, but for an incident that could have ended in fatal injury. After some hours of exhausting and cautious patrolling my group, consisting of four soldiers and myself, came across a cow shed on the way back to camp and we decided to have a rest. We lay down on the straw in one corner of the shed, the rest of which housed two cows. One chap held guard, the rest almost immediately fell asleep. I happened to lie further away from the corner. Suddenly I was woken up by a tremendous shriek - it appeared that the guard looked into the shed at the very moment when one of the cows having moved towards me, was an inch away from me with her rear leg about to step on my face. A very lucky escape indeed!

It was now the beginning of March and the weather was

changing rapidly. Nights were still quite cold, but days became longer, bright and sunny. Spring was unmistakably in the air. As much as one enjoyed the change, our task became more difficult, for we had to be much more careful in daylight than under cover of darkness. Whilst the situation on the Eastern front had been changing rapidly and the enemy had been pushed back from towns and villages in the Soviet Union, on the Western Front, things were static, and it appeared as if the German Command resolved to dig in its heels and not to move an inch.

Towards the end of March and during April some small changes in the distribution of our Units took place. Without being told one felt that fairly soon we would be going into action. In the meantime our Battalion, and presumably other Battalions as well, was moved very close to the enemy line and its task was to take over advance positions from units of the British Army.

These advance positions were a number of bunkers in the hill slopes. About 50 feet away from these dugouts there was a low stone wall, the kind of which was often used to divide field parcels. If you crept up to that wall and took out a stone from the middle, which was very easy to do for the wall was built by piling stone upon stone, then you could see German machine gun posts, and occasionally, the changing of observers.

Since I spoke English and was an officer cadet with one bar to my epaulettes - the usual rank one was promoted to after successfully completing the Officer Cadet Course - I was assigned to take over one of the bunkers from a British lieutenant.

He could hardly hide his delight at the thought of being relieved. He very politely and very briefly described the situation. He told me that the German positions were only a few hundred yards away, that their observers watch us very carefully and open fire at the slightest movement by us, therefore, he stressed, there must be no activity that might rouse their suspicion. It is essential - he said - that in daylight one should keep low to the ground and only at night one could stretch oneself.

About a quarter of a mile away from the bunker, down at the bottom of the valley through which one had to approach the ridge with the bunker, there was a well. The officer pointed it out to me and said that water could be drawn from it, but only at night, provided you crept down to the well very quietly.

Any noticeable movement would inevitably provoke a salvo from the Nebelwerfer, a multiple rocket launcher, initially used for smoke screens, but adapted to throw rockets, six of them at once, to cover a wide area. This piece of artillery was most demoralising, for it lit up the sky and made a cutting, swishing frightening noise.

I took in the information with a sinking feeling in my stomach, caused as much by what the officer told me as by a strong stench which pervaded the air in the bunker. I plucked up courage and asked him what was the source of that strong smell. 'O! that' he said 'a dead body lying outside - he has been there for some time'. When I asked him why the body hadn't been buried, he grimaced slightly as if expressing annoyance at my questioning him, and said that he would not expose his men to danger; besides, the Canadians, the Indians and others had been here and they did not bury him, so why should we do it.

This sounded to me very cynical and inconsiderate and I decided that as soon as we took over, we should try to perform the duty to the dead. However, after the first two days of our keeping vigil, we realised the danger involved, and regrettably behaved no better than our predecessors.

For a fortnight I and my group of nine 'lived' on our bellies. We crawled during the day to our observation posts, from which we could clearly see a large number of dead bodies spread over the area dividing us from the enemy positions, we crawled back to the bunker for water and food, moved extremely cautiously a few steps away from the bunker to a spot for toilet purposes, collected a bucketful of water at night and counted the days with profound longing to the moment of relief.

Eventually it came and we returned to base. A proper wash and a decent meal - what a delight! It is difficult to appreciate these blessings unless one is exposed to hardship the kind of which we experienced that fortnight.

Provision and munitions for the people holding the advanced positions had to be supplied by carriers and only at night and in silence, so as not to be detected by the enemy patrols and observers. After a few days at the base, I was asked by my Company Commander to lead a group of carriers to the advanced posts. The distance was about two miles and the way along a winding path through a grove, some pastures, shrubs and up a hill. Parts of the path were indicated by a narrow, white ribbon, only just noticeable in the dark.

I had a group of twelve, some carrying food, some ammunition in their fully packed rucksacks. The sky was moonless but clear and the air pleasantly cool. After the routine check and reminder about the absolute necessity of walking one behind the other with 2 to 3 meters between in complete silence and with great care, the Company Commander sent us on our way.

The first quarter of a mile was easy going and one was lulled into complacency, but soon it became much harder. The undergrowth became dense and treading on twigs and breaking stems inevitably generated noise. To compound the difficulties the sky clouded over and it became quite dark. Tiredness and concentration imposed a constantly growing strain. I stopped and ordered a rest. We dared not sit down for fear of making a noise, so everybody just stood, slipped the luggage off their shoulders and rested. A few minutes later we continued.

The main problem was finding the white ribboned path and

this turned out to be more difficult than I thought. We must have deviated somewhat from the intended path. When, in my scouts days, I was told that it is possible to find one's direction by the position of the Great Bear and the North Star, I somehow never believed that one could really find oneself in a situation when the only help would come from that celestial body. Luckily, the sky cleared and the Great Bear appeared in all its majesty.

I had to head duly North and I had been out quite a few degrees. Anxious not to show nervousness and indecision, I started correcting the direction hoping to find the white ribbon. The next ten minutes or so were as long as eternity, but suddenly a white thin line appeared on the ground. We were saved.

There was still a distance of about three quarters of a mile to go when all of a sudden the sky lit up and shells were exploding, at first at some distance in front of us, but seconds later, dangerously close to us. Suddenly two shells landed and exploded within a few feet from our group. Three chaps were wounded, one severely: a shrapnel cut a deep wound in his back. Since we had no stretcher-bearer with us or anyone trained to dress wounds, I performed the duty with some trepidation, hoping that it would be possible to get him to base before he lost too much blood. The line of fire moved on further away from us and after a minute, stopped. It was quiet again and I looked round to assess the situation.

Most of the group dispersed; the wounded soldier, two others and myself remained. I left one chap to look after the wounded and the remaining one and myself continued our journey with whatever luggage we managed to carry. When we arrived at our destination we were told how it all started. One of our soldiers on duty at an observation point noticed unusual movements on the German positions. Instead of one or two soldiers slipping out or into their bunker, he saw a machine gun being taken out from the bunker and a few men with guns and grenades spreading out and aiming their rifles directly at him. Overcome with fear, he opened fire. In reply the Germans lay a barrage of mortar and light artillery guns, covering some of our advanced positions but also the area further away. As it happened we were the only ones to have casualties.

It was a case of a man brought to the verge of endurance by exhaustion and lack of sleep. His imagination played him up and his nerves no longer could take the strain. Luckily we got away with relatively light injuries. There was no sympathy for us from our comrades on the first line, for they expected food and cigarettes but neither came.

The Commander ordered two men to go with me to get the wounded soldier back to base. Dawn was breaking when we arrived at the point where the wounded man rested. Remarkably, in spite of a heavy loss of blood and great pain, he was quite composed. We managed to get him to base and we passed him over to the care of the Base doctor. All of my group were accounted for, but most of the luggage had been dropped while running away from the exploding bombs. There was a question of recovering it, but since that could only be done at night, success was very problematic and the idea was abandoned.

A strange atmosphere pervaded the Base. It was obvious to everybody that the day of reckoning was close, but no one, at least of the lower ranks, knew what form the action would take, which group or Company would go where and what sort of resistance we might expect. There was an uneasy calm and even the most imaginative and talkative among us stopped speculating. We had very little knowledge of previous actions, though we knew that before us there were here other troops who were engaged in battle.

No details were revealed to us for obvious reasons. We now know that the hills our Battalion was facing, in particular, Hill 593, the highest in that range, were attacked in February '44 by the Royal Sussex with fatal results, then there were further unsuccessful actions by Hindu and Maori Battalions with even heavier losses.

The enemy defended the Gustav line, a formidable range of bunkers and observation posts dominating the surrounding area and stretching from the peak Monte Cairo to the Monastery Monte Cassino, and the Hitler line, covering the area from Monte Cairo to Piedimonte, Ponte Corvo and St. Oliva.

It must have been known to the upper echelons what had been said on the BBC in a talk about the war on the 23 March 1944 i.e.: 'It is beyond doubt that the Germans have concentrated crack troops at Cassino for whom only the very best Allied troops can be a match.'

A frightfully costly lesson from previous actions had been learned by the Allies and a grim decision must have been taken to put into the next battle every possible resource, every effort, to win. And indeed a consolidated Allied action, involving troops of several nationalities serving under British Command, as well as several divisions of American forces, had been planned. The Polish Corps was given the responsibility of defending the segment at Cassino.

It was May already and early summer came in a blaze of flowers with the predominance of poppies, defiantly asserting their presence on the shell-scarred slopes of the hills near the Monte Cassino Monastery. The sight was unreal and incongruous: shattered tree trunks with sharp broken branches reaching out accusingly to the sky and a fresh, soft, dew-bathed meadow with a multitude of wild flowers in the valley. This stretch of land had already carried memories of several bloody, unsuccessful assaults on German positions. Its undergrowth had been concealing bodies of men killed in the battles with no immediate prospects of burial because of the watchful eyes of the enemy. No chivalry and no compassion here. Any attempt to collect a dead body from that area would have immediately drawn enemy fire. For weeks there had been a steady, continuous war of attrition. Both sides knew exactly each other's positions and regular shelling went on all the time. The slightest movement triggered off enemy reaction. The Germans used mortars and the multibarrel Nebelwerfers which, at first struck terror into the hearts of our troops, for they would spew out a dozen or so shells with a frightful noise, causing devastation over a large area. With time we got used to that high pitched sound and would have considered it unusual if it had stopped.

To everybody's surprise we were ordered to wear trainers instead of boots. On the 11th of May in the morning orders came to collect additional ammunition and emergency rations - a clear indication of impending action. It was hazy and dull and only towards midday the sun broke through and the contours of the hills round the Monastery appeared from the mist. The walls of the Monastery, which had been partly damaged in previous bombings, threateningly dominated the horizon. There was a strange and somewhat mysterious atmosphere, for, most unusually, shelling from both sides stopped and the silence became oppressive. Only towards the evening a little sporadic firing from our artillery took place as if to reassure that everything was normal. Later in the evening, under cover of darkness, my Company was moved from the Base, in small groups and with extreme caution, towards the foot of Hill 593, which, as mentioned before, was the highest peak in the hills close to the Monastery. Hill 593 was nature's ideal gift to the defender, for it had chines, crevices and boulders.

THE BATTLE FOR THE MONASTERY

In addition there were here ruins of an old fort with a good supply of chunks of masonry. Having crept up in silence to the foot of the hill, we took up positions from which we were to go into attack with the object of dislodging the Germans from their bunkers on the other side of the hill.

It must have been well after midnight when our artillery opened fire and laid a barrage on the German line of defence. In response a hail of machine gun bullets, hand grenades and mortar shells showered over the field in front of us. We were waiting for the order to move. There was grim determination on the faces of the men. Flashes from German rockets were lighting up the hill in an effort to enable their sharp shooters from around the Monastery and other positions to aim at our troops. The ground was trembling from bomb explosions and it seemed impossible to advance a step.

We spread out and lay on the ground waiting. I do not remember having any thought in my mind, neither do I recall any emotion, neither fear nor bravery. Suddenly there was a break in the shooting and my platoon Commander gave an order to advance. No sooner did we make a few steps up the hill when a salvo of enemy fire covered the ground. We must have been quite close to the enemy bunkers for hand grenades began to explode around us.

I threw myself to the ground and suddenly I felt a piercing

pain in my buttock. I touched it and felt blood. We got up and ran forward covering the field with fire from our tommy guns throwing grenades and taking up a position for a machine gun. We succeeded in getting up to the top of the hill and to position the machine gun. It was an unbelievably simple operation and for a while I wondered why there was so much fuss with the preparations. But suddenly hell broke loose. Grenades were exploding, tracer bullets were cutting the receding darkness before dawn like a glowing sword, and hitting targets. One of the first to die from a tracer bullet lodged in the head was my Company Commander - a scene I shall never forget. Shells were exploding killing and maiming our men. Two platoon Commanders and a dozen men were killed and about 30 wounded in the first few minutes after the early conquest of Hill 593, among them four of my group of 12. We still had the machine gun and we covered our segment with fire quite effectively. Dawn was breaking and in the dim daylight a scene of horror unfolded: blood covered bodies, people with shot off legs, broken arms. I saw it only in a flash, the scene did not sink in, for our eyes were fixed on the enemy position and the undergrowth from which fire was coming. Then it happened. A hand grenade landed a foot or so from the two men serving our machine gun, killed one outright and fatally injured the other. I was hit with a shower of small pieces of the shell along my left arm and leg and momentarily deafened by the explosion. I took over the machine gun and kept the position with the remaining four men. The pain didn't worry me, but I began to lose blood and felt weak. This must have been noticed by my platoon Commander, who ordered me to try to withdraw to base.

I passed on the machine gun to two men of my greatly depleted team and began to think how to make my way back to the Base. The danger of being picked up by a sniper was very real and the ground around us was still receiving sporadic bombs. One could not safely stand up. I faced an alternative: either to slide forward into the shrub covered ground from which not long ago enemy fire was coming, but which for some time had remained quiet, possibly indicating that the Germans had withdrawn, or crawling back up the hill and letting myself down the slope towards our auxiliary units. The former was a risky unknown, the latter carried the danger of exposing oneself to the eye of a sniper from the Monastery.

I decided to choose the former course and slowly moved forward sliding on my belly down the hill into the overgrown ground. On the way down I noticed a few injured men lying on the ground, among them some in German battledress. Shooting was going on all the time, but I was indifferent to that and tried to get into the shrubs as imperceptibly and as quickly as possible. What happened next is blank in my memory. I must have passed out and been picked up by that absolutely remarkable stretcher bearer, Brzezinski, who under fire, being himself wounded, went from one casualty to another, applying dressings, dragging wounded out to relative safety, comforting and saving lives.

Next, I remember being carried to the Doctor's House and put on an improvised operating table, turned unceremoniously on my belly and subjected to a very painful procedure of picking out bits of iron from my side and buttock. I could not help noticing the somewhat flippant attitude of the surgeon, as though to say that my wounds were trivial and I shouldn't have wasted his time. He had full rights to entertain such a notion for in the operating room were already several limbless men and some with severe head and back injuries.

Some hours later I was carried further back to the Base and from there I was evacuated the following day to the military Hospital, probably at Campobasso. There I found out more about what happened on Hill 593 after I had left.

There were no fewer than six counterattacks by the Germans, each exacting tremendous casualties in our Battalion. My Company was virtually wiped out and the other two Companies fared very little better. After ten hours of mutual slaughter, for the Germans suffered heavy losses too, we were pushed back down hill and only a reinforced, consolidated assault on the 17th May brought decisive victory. The Germans were in complete retreat and the Polish flag was proudly hoisted on the roof of the Monastery.

The Battle of Monte Cassino has been described in several books (Fred Majdalany(l), Melchior Wankowicz(2) and others) and there is a consensus of opinion that it was one of the bloodiest in the war. Out of 12 Infantry Battalions and three Cavalry Brigades my Battalion (The 2nd) was in the second place after the 18th, in the list of casualties(2). After the collapse of the Gustav line and the Hitler line the road to Rome was open. The conquest of Monte Cassino was a turning point in the fortunes of the Allied actions in Italy.

MY FRIEND JUREK

Since my Battalion left Lebanon for Palestine my personal contact with Jurek was broken and we kept in touch by correspondence. Strict secrecy was kept with regard to location of army units and letters were usually addressed to the person and his Battalion. It was surprising that letters reached their destination, but they did and hardly any got lost in spite of frequent movements of various units. We both were conscious of the requirement that no information which could remotely be useful to the enemy should be written in letters and so generalities of a personal nature were the subject of our correspondence, a prominent part of which was taken up with reports on amorous adventures.

Since we both had by then a rudimentary knowledge of Italian and could chat up signorinas in their own language, we fared reasonably well in romantic affairs and it was always pleasant and safe to write about that.

When my Battalion moved closer to the front our correspondence ceased because the usual post facilities had been reduced to a minimum and sending private letters virtually stopped. Jurek had been in a headquarter unit on a relatively safe job, well away from immediate danger. I often thought about him and wished we could get together again for a chat. About a fortnight after the event at Monte Cassino I found myself in a transport of wounded to Casamassima, a small village in the south of Italy where there was a large rehabilitation army Hospital.

The atmosphere there was relaxed and the care of residents magnificent. One tended to forget that the war was still going on and the battles for the rest of Italy were fierce. I was recovering from my wounds quite quickly and started getting up and venturing out from my ward. There was a certain amount of movement of patients between wards and I got to know and became friendly with Simon, a former Grammar School teacher of French. He was older than me but from the very beginning of our acquaintance there was a measure of empathy between us. One afternoon while visiting me, he told me that in his ward there was a student from Cracow, who had been severely wounded. Out of idle curiosity I asked him what subject did that student study? Law - he said. "What's his name?" Jurek W. - was the answer.

I was stunned. I immediately decided to walk over to his ward to see him. The reunion was emotional but we both kept a stiff upper lip. Jurek lost one leg. The story is short and very sad. Right through the action at Monte Cassino his unit had been well behind the danger zone: it was garrisoned in a small village and it had at no time been exposed to enemy attack. One Sunday morning a number of soldiers, amongst them Jurek, were standing round in the market place of the village, talking. Suddenly two enemy aircraft appeared, dived and opened fire on the group of soldiers. The result: Jurek's left leg was virtually shot off and one other soldier was lightly wounded. There followed an amputation high up his leg, leaving a very short stump.

As long as I stayed in the Hospital I visited him daily. I admired his composure, though it was obvious to me that he suppressed a deep feeling of anxiety and sadness. Luckily, the people on the Ward were very friendly to him, two in particular, who, with one other from a neighbouring Ward, made up a bridge party. That must have helped a great deal since it diverted his attention from the state he was in and concentrated his mind on the game. He used to tell me how very kind the Ward sister was to him and how much he appreciated the warmth and friendship of the nursing staff.

I was recovering quickly except for some trouble with my left ear which was damaged by the blast of the explosion. I was still under treatment, but was allowed to wander round in the quite extensive grounds of the Hospital. There was an opportunity to meet people, to discuss serious matters or just socialise.

Some information reached us about the progress of the war, but none at all about what was happening in occupied Europe. Little did I know that by then practically all European Jewry except some miserable remnants of tortured humanity still incarcerated in concentration camps, had vanished. No one among us had the slightest idea of what was actually going on in Poland and there was no way to find out. We now know that one or two people managed to escape from Poland and travel to London to tell the British authorities about the atrocities committed by the Nazis in the Ghettos, about the deliberate policy of complete annihilation of the Jews in occupied Europe, but this news was received with incredulity and looked upon as anti-German propaganda.

The Allied Forces were successful in their march Northwards but were encountering stiff enemy resistance. We, in the relatively safe South, were following closely the progress and were hoping for a speedy end of the war. But that was not to be for almost another full year.

The German propaganda was boosting the morale of their Forces with the announcement of a new and devastating weapon, the V-1 Flying bomb, and the first attack of that frightening bomb on Britain took place on the 13th June 1944. Though this weapon caused a great deal of damage and numerous casualties, it did not manage to shake the morale of people, in particular, the Londoners, who were first to suffer from it. There was a feeling that the war was being won though one had learned to be cautious with predictions.

ALLIED FORCES IN ROME

On the 4th of June 1944 Allied Forces entered Rome. This was a tremendous blow to the German defence effort and a most significant achievement for the Allies. I left the Hospital after about two months and I returned to my Battalion, which was by now beyond recognition. Most of the people I went to battle with at Monte Cassino were missing, the larger part of those were dead, the rest wounded, some severely, some recuperating with the hope of returning to their Companies. Soon after my return to active service I was notified that I had been commissioned and made an officer, a humble second lieutenant. That one pip made a great difference in the way of life of a soldier. Smarter uniform, officers mess, being saluted by the other ranks, more money and the service of a valet.

It was too dramatic a change and it took me some time to get used to the privileges of my new status. My Battalion was now kept in reserve and the duties were mainly training and garrison routine. I was now given the task of supply officer, which in practice meant to arrange for the provision of uniforms, boots, underwear from Headquarters. This made me sometime unpopular with the H.Q. Officers but it had the advantage of giving me freedom to travel and to use my initiative, albeit within narrow limits.

'HOLIDAYS' IN EGYPT

After some time in the Hospital in Cassamassima I discovered that the most coveted place for a holiday for some officers was Cairo. No doubt the Egyptian metropolis had plenty of attractions: the universal use of English, the by now security from invasion, but first of all the abundance of cabarets and bordellos. But there was something else that was a powerful reason for the choice of Egypt for a holiday. It was a secret and only by chance did I discover the nature of that secret.

When I left the hospital I asked for a fortnight's leave with the intention of spending it in Rome. I mentioned my plan to a young doctor whom I got to know at the Hospital. He cogitated for a while and asked why I didn't want to go to Egypt for my holiday since, not only would I be able to cover all my expenses but also make some money. 'It is simple' he said. 'When you are in Cairo go to any bank and buy gold sovereigns, at £1 a piece, and bring them back. Here you will sell them for £10 each. There is nothing to it - some people have made fortunes' he said, 'and if you do go don't forget to buy some for me'.

I didn't go and I missed 'making a fortune', but what my friend told me was very true, as I later found out. There was a substantial flow of gold sovereigns (cryptically called 'chestnuts') into Italy through the agency of 'holiday' makers, who accumulated considerable sums of money. This was, of course, illegal but the trade went on just the same for a long time and the 'secret' became almost public knowledge.

There was a sinister side to the whole business: apparently some of this gold found its way across the battle front into Germany. Rumours had it that one of the British Quartermasters took the wages of a whole Battalion to Egypt, bought chestnuts' and was about to become a millionaire when, unfortunately, he was caught with the load of gold coins on his way back from his holiday and arrested.

MY HOLIDAY IN ROME

The delightful feeling of well-being after recovery from an illness is generally known. All physical manifestations of the regained strength come into play: a voracious appetite, a desire to exert oneself, to run, to push one's limits of physical endurance further than one's recorded experience, and of course, the sexual desire takes dominance, often to the exclusion of other needs, particularly if one is in his early twenties.

At the convalescent Hospital there were attractive nurses, but very few compared with the number of men, and naturally, competition was fierce. My relations with the weaker sex under the prevailing conditions was limited to an exchange of pleasantries.

It was common knowledge that the only available way of satisfying sexual urge was during periodic leave at bordellos. In spite of frequent reminders of the danger of infection and notwithstanding the order to collect condoms from the Medical Centre before going on holiday, there had been cases of venereal infections and a special clinic was established to cater for such patients. Numerous jokes were circulating concerning that clinic and apparently the receptionist, an Italian woman, used to greet a prospective patient with the straight-to-the point question: 'Pipa piange?' - does the pipe weep?'

I was looking forward to going to Rome about which I knew

only as much as I could remember from my school days. I wanted to visit the Vatican, the Colosseum, the Palazzo Venezia and other famous places, and of course, to see the Pope. There was no public transport to Rome from where we stayed. One way of getting there was to go to the nearest British Army Airport and catch a lift. I managed to get to the Airport in an Army lorry, and lo and behold, a bomber with a dozen British soldiers was about to leave for Rome.

It was now a question of finding accommodation for a fortnight, which turned out to be easier than I expected. There was a Polish Army club where one could get information about accommodation and the one I took turned out to be very conveniently situated. It was within walking distance to the centre and most of the objects I wished to see and places I wished to visit. The landlady was very pleasant and helpful and the room comfortable. I was duly impressed by the Colosseum and reminded of its inglorious history, I admired the Fountain di Trevi, its god Oceanus riding in a conch shell drawn by two horses, visited Palazzo Venezia and stood on the balcony from which Mussolini roused the crowd to frenzy, went to the Vatican and waited for hours to see the Pope being carried shoulder high in a lectus (sedan chair).

Little did I know at the time how indifferent the Pope, Pius the XII, was to the planned, systematic and cold-blooded murder of Jews, including the Italian Jewish community, by the Nazis with the collaboration of the Italian fascists. His past service as Nunzio in Germany must have had something to do with his attitude.

My 'cultural' activities were pleasantly complemented by an unusually lucky set of circumstances. My landlady had a niece staying with her, a pretty girl of twenty, who spoke a little English but was very patient with my Italian and who offered to accompany me on several of my trips in town. Soon a romantic relationship developed which blossomed right through my stay in Rome. A perfect holiday.

VICTORY IN EUROPE (VE-DAY)

I was still on my holiday in Rome when the news broke of the German force's surrender to General Eisenhower. A day later, the 8th May 1945, war in Europe was declared over and VE-Day was celebrated throughout Britain and some countries on the Continent. In Rome the news of the end of war was received with satisfaction and serenity but there was no manifestation of exuberant joy as in Britain. On returning from my holiday I resumed my duties at the Battalion H.Q.

More news from Poland became available and gradually the tragic picture of devastation, destruction and mass murder unfolded before our eyes.

It was difficult to believe that millions of civilians, women and children were enslaved in concentration camps in a deliberate, cold blooded, meticulously planned action of mass murder through torture, starvation, and gas chambers. The thought was beyond perception, the facts incredulous.

It took a long time and much evidence to convince oneself that these events in occupied Poland were true. The joy of victory was drowned in sadness and sorrow for our dearest. It didn't seem to be right to celebrate.

The initial longing to return home to my family was now dulled by doubt and despair. No one I loved and cherished was alive. The whole country receded in my mind into permanent darkness. A feeling of alienation and even hostility to what was once my country ensued.

Having been liberated by the Red Army, Poland was now completely dependent on the generosity of the Soviet Union, which decided not only upon the type of Government the country should have but also on security, social problems, industry, etc. In a word, every aspect of life was patterned on the Soviet model.

At times I thought that perhaps one problem that assumed almost critical dimensions in Poland in the thirties i.e. growing anti-Semitism might now have vanished or, at least, diminished. Regrettably, this was not the case and manifestations of hostility to the survivors of the holocaust and the few thousands Jews who returned to Poland from the war stricken Soviet Union were unmistakably evident.

AN HOUR OF REMEMBRANCE

The summer sun was setting behind the Apennines flooding the horizon with orange and red. It was the 11th of May 1945, the first anniversary of arguably the war's bloodiest battle, that for the Monte Cassino Monastery and the road to Rome. My Battalion was assembled on a large field in front of our tents and its three Companies stood in a 'U' shape formation. In front of each Company stood its Commander with a Register in his hands. There was complete silence.

The darkness which quickly spread round after sunset was pierced by a few flickering torches. The solemn silence was broken by the voice of the Commander who was calling out the names of soldiers who fell in battle. After each name called out there was a short pause and then the Sergeant-major of the particular Company answered: 'Polegl na polu chwaly', literally, 'fell in the field of glory', or simply, 'killed in action'.

Among those were eight young and healthy men from my group of twelve, and that was approximately the proportion of killed in the whole fighting Battalion. Out of the remaining four two were wounded and only two came out unscathed. It was difficult to overcome the deep sorrow at the loss of one's friends and comrades.

To those six I added in commemoration, privately and in silence, the loss of ten members of my closest family.

By now the enormity of the tragic events in Poland, the

holocaust, became known. The annihilation of European Jewry by slave labour and in gas chambers at Auschwitz and other concentration camps was now common knowledge, but the reaction to these events by my comrades-in-arms was muted. They were embarrassed to talk about it, either for fear of getting emotionally involved or for lack of interest.

A NEW PERSPECTIVE

Winning the war meant for most soldiers a long awaited return home: British to Britain, Americans to the USA, French to France, but not so for us in the Polish Forces.

The option of return existed, but there was a well justified fear that on returning to the country soldiers of the Anders army, as we were generally spoken of, would be interrogated, accused of right wing convictions, and at best looked upon and treated with contempt by officialdom, at worst detained for some imaginary political crimes.

Only a few expressed a wish to return to Poland, the bulk preferred to wait for a different solution to the problem of demobilisation.

The only alternative was to remain for some undefined time in British care until a more permanent solution is found.

An atmosphere of inertia prevailed. I felt I must decide what to do with myself without waiting for others to decide for me. Just before the war broke out I had finished the third year of Chemistry, a subject I liked and was reasonably good at. But now, I thought, how much do I remember and am I now capable of taking up the threads and carrying on?

Doubts were gnawing away at my morale. I had sleepless nights not being able to decide, but then information reached me that some 'unfinished' students from other Polish Units were allowed to carry on with their studies at one of the two

Universities in Beirut. Those were medical students, and again I wondered whether this possibility was also open for other studies. I decided to apply for permission to continue my studies, and to my surprise, the response was prompt and positive.

It was now a question of transport to Lebanon. Things were coming my way. I did not have to wait long. Within a month I found myself in a transport of soldiers and some Polish families on the way to Lebanon.

Now the question was to be accepted by the American University for continuation of my studies. I had to reconcile myself with the possibility of having to repeat a year or two of my course of studies, to refresh my memory and to adjust to an undoubtedly different system from that I was used to at Cracow University.

But first I had to produce evidence that I was a University student and how much of the Chemistry course I had covered.

I decided to write to Cracow University with a request for the requisite document, and again to my delight, within a few weeks I received a very friendly letter with the requested document. Armed with this document I applied to the American University and was accepted to the second year of Chemistry.

There had been already in Beirut a substantial number of Polish families who came from Russia and also a few dozen ex servicemen who fought at Tobruk and other places of the North

African front. These were mainly medical students, who were continuing their studies at the French University.

There was a kind of Polish Consular Authority which looked after the Polish families, providing them with accommodation, food and most essential necessities and also kept a paternal eye on the students. Ex-servicemen students fared generally better than others since they were still being paid by the Army.

The majority of students lived in one large house called 'the students house'. It was therefore easy to get to know many of them and to make friends.

Strolling in the University campus I recalled the experience from about three years before when I and my friend, Jurek, passing by an open door of a large room with beautiful pictures on walls, ventured in uninvited, and astonishingly, were accorded a very friendly reception by the wife of the President of the University. I also remembered my thoughts which were how lovely it would have been if I could continue my studies in that serene and attractive environment. I felt grateful for the fulfilment of my wish.

LEBANON

How refreshing this country was! What a beautiful stretch of land between snow covered mountains and glistening sea! The change was dramatic and held the promise of a normal and pleasant life.

I had very little knowledge about the country and decided to learn something about its political and social life, but first I had to concentrate on getting adjusted to the 'student's mode' of life. The routine of attending lectures and laboratory work was easily absorbed but it was at first mechanical and I experienced difficulties in memorising formulae and descriptive matter. I had always been better at reasoning than memorising and now I had to train my memory by using associations and mnemonics.

After the defeat of the Ottoman Empire by Britain and France in the first World War, the League of Nations gave France a mandate over the area that is now Syria and Lebanon. In 1941 Lebanon was proclaimed an independent Republic by the Free French. French rule had generally a very beneficial effect on the culture and economy of the country. Literacy in Lebanon at that time was higher than in any other Middle East country. There was a high proportion of schools, both general and technical as well as agricultural colleges.

The population consisted of Maronite Christians and Moslems, roughly in equal numbers, and a sizeable community of Druses living mainly in villages in the Lebanese mountains.

There were many French schools and schools run by Americans who had lived in the country for many years. The American University of Beirut (AUB) was founded by Quakers in the late 1800s and much the same time the French Université, St. Joseph, came into existence. The Polish contingent of students was divided between these two Universities with a large proportion of medical students studying at the French University.

What struck me from the very beginning of my stay was the comparatively large number of official holidays. That was, as I found later, an official Government decision to respect the religious sensibilities of both communities, the Christian and Muslim. The system by which deputies were chosen to the Parliament, that is, the Chamber of Deputies, was called 'confessional representation' and was based on religion: each religious sect elected a representative in proportion to its size.

Surprisingly, this system worked well for many years and there was peaceful coexistence between the two major communities. It sounds incredible in view of the terrible bloodshed that happened in recent years. After some months of intensive studies and adjustment to civilian life I began to enjoy my new environment.

The University campus was large, clean, beautifully kept, adorned with an abundance of flowers and shaded by magnificent cedars. I remembered that King Solomon brought cedars from Lebanon to use in the building of the Temple. My colleagues at the University were Lebanese, Syrians, a sprinkling of Egyptians and some Armenians, and of course, some Poles. They were all friendly and though most were quite a few years younger than I was, we got on very well.

The teachers at the Chemistry Department were four professors: two Americans, one Greek and one Lebanese. In addition to the obligatory subjects for an honours degree in Chemistry one had to take an additional subject to comply with the requirements. I chose History of Philosophy. I had always been mildly interested in philosophy and had hoped to gain some knowledge in this subject. However, my choice turned out to be unfortunate, for the lecturer, the Lebanese, was an old, short legged fat man, always wearing a fez and walking fast and unevenly like a rolling rugby ball. He liked to tell jokes and hardly ever gave a proper lecture. He would mention a philosophical term or phrase such as, for instance, what is the 'Ontological argument?' and would go round the class asking everybody what was meant by it.

Naturally a number of interpretations were produced, and since he did not bother to give a conclusive answer to the question, we remained no wiser than before the session. The American professor, Bill West, was pleasant, friendly, a keen tennis player, but somewhat distant and always very fair in assessing a student's achievement. The Greek professor, Christofus, was serious and sombre, aloof and conscious of his position, somewhat disgruntled, probably because he was not made Dean of the Department.

The Academic day at the AUB always started with an Assembly of students in the Chapel and a talk with some moral or spiritual content given by a lecturer. This 'service' was interdenominational so that everybody, irrespective of one's religion, could take part in it.

One day I was greatly surprised to discover that there were at the AUB several Israeli students, that is, Jewish students from what was then still Palestine. They were studying medicine and I met two of them in the chemical laboratory. I spoke to them in Hebrew and I found out what the current political situation was in Palestine. This was towards the end of 1947 when the atmosphere in Palestine was already highly charged. They told me that very soon they would not be allowed into Lebanon for the hostility of Arabs to Jews was rising from day to day.

There were some signs of anti-Semitism in Lebanon too but none could yet be discerned at the University. Life went on pleasantly and uneventfully.

One afternoon stuck in my mind particularly vividly. I was sitting with friends at the dinner table at Halabi's Restaurant, a reasonably priced eating place with some reductions for students, when our liaison officer came in, sat down at the table and announced in a somewhat formal way that H.Q. had sent him a Cross of Valour (Krzyz Walecznych) to be handed over to me. There were congratulations all round. It would be insincere on my part not to admit that I was pleased or even a little proud. Had I still been with my Battalion in Italy, this medal would have been pinned on my chest by a general or at least a colonel at a solemn ceremony. That's how the others received their medals. Instead I had to be satisfied to receive it from a humble lieutenant while munching my lunch. The occasion brought back memories, some from well before the action in Italy.

It was somewhere in the Middle East at one of our training camps. After a hard slogging morning we were resting in tents sheltered from the hot sun. Some chaps complained in crude soldier language about the sergeant who chased us unnecessarily up the hill with a full load on our backs, others took this effort stoically. Then one of my colleagues, Stan Lasota, unexpectedly and irrelevantly said 'I would give my arm for a Cross of Valour'. Stan gave his life in battle and had not even been awarded a posthumous Cross of Valour. He was one of hundreds killed in action whose reward were simple wooden crosses on their graves at the Monte Cassino military cemetery.

It also reminded me of the extraordinary and crazy bravery of officer cadet Liberman who, after having received a bullet which lodged in his thigh, stayed on and defended his position. Some minutes later he was wounded again by shrapnel. He managed to crawl into a bunker and bandage his bleeding wound; he stayed there for a while but decided to return to his post. By an incredible effort he crawled out and inched his way to his previous position, when suddenly he was hit by a shower of pieces from an enemy hand grenade which put an end to his life. Killed in stages. Did he get a medal posthumously? Probably not. He was one of many.

Beirut, the capital, a city of nearly half a million was the Mecca for the Middle East rich Arabs who used to come to it not to pray but to spend their money at luxury hotels, cabarets and brothels of which there was an abundance.

I spent part of my summer vacation at a student's holiday camp in the Lebanese mountains, close to a Druse village, part in Palestine - there was still free movement between the two countries, but most of it on the most attractive beach in Beirut.

By then I had made many friends, some of whom were girl-fellow students. Their number was much smaller than that of men and a sizeable proportion of them lived with their families. They came from what is conventionally spoken of 'good families', were well behaved, had gentle manners and expected courteous behaviour from the opposite sex. There were a few who experienced very hard conditions while living with their families in God forsaken places in the Soviet Union. They were then teenagers and their education was unavoidably interrupted. It called for a considerable effort to make up for lost time in order to qualify for university studies. There were a few who survived the war in Poland and managed somehow to get out after the war and to continue their secondary education followed by university studies.

I met one of these lucky girls. Her name was Helena. She had blue eyes and blond flowing hair and because of her non stereotypically Jewish looks, she succeeded in avoiding being shut in the Warsaw Ghetto. Helena and her brother who was three years younger than her, were looked after by a peasant family in a village not far from Warsaw. That was a commercial transaction costing their parents everything they possessed. They themselves were taken away with thousands of others to Treblinka or Auschwitz.

Helena studied Chemistry, she was doing the first year, and I used to see her in the Analytical laboratory. Our friendship developed slowly and grew stronger with time. We had a great deal in common and always had a lot to talk about. I admired her relationship with her brother, who soon after the war ended, managed, thanks to old friends of their parents, to go to what was still then Palestine, where assistance was given to him to continue his education. She always addressed him as my little son. The English translation of the Polish diminutive does not adequately convey the love and warmth of the expression. She was told by her parents to look after the little boy and she dutifully and lovingly fulfilled their wish.

There were times of great happiness in our relationship, exaltation and rapture, moments of deep conviction that we were destined for each other. Then, almost suddenly, without reason the emotional horizon would cloud over and a feeling of sadness and emptiness would set in. We were both unhappy about the sudden change but it appeared as though we could not prevent it happening.

The beginning of the 1948 academic year was marked by some unpleasant signs. The events in Palestine reverberated outside her borders in the Arab world. There were anti-Jewish demonstrations in Beirut and the propaganda spilled over onto University territory. There were no longer any Jewish students from Palestine and rumours were circulating that pressure was being exerted on the University authorities to dismiss Jewish students irrespective of origin and prohibit them from entering the campus. The Polish Students Union hastily called a meeting at which the current events in Palestine were debated, and to its eternal shame, its Committee drafted a resolution to be voted on by the whole assembly stating that the Union 'does not support, nor does it recognise Jewish aspirations to an independent State and expresses solidarity with the Arabs'. This, I thought, was outrageous. I rose and said that the Union was a non-political organisation and had no mandate to express political opinions and such a resolution would be in breach of the Union's Constitution. Regrettably, I had very little support. The resolution was passed by a large majority. Anti-Semitism which lay dormant under the surface came to life. The traditional Jew-haters scored a double: they expressed their anti-Semitism and they reaffirmed their sycophantic attitude to the Lebanese.

Later that year I was advised not to attend lectures and not to venture onto the campus. By then I had already passed all degree examinations except one major in Physical Chemistry and one minor, in Organic Analysis.

The lecturer in Physical Chemistry was Prof. West who was also Dean of the Department. I was in a quandary and did not know what to do to rescue the result of all my effort. I decided to write to Prof. West. A few days later I had a letter from him asking me to see him at his private address. To my astonishment and delight he suggested that I come to his house twice a week for private tuition in order to complete the course in Physical Chemistry and with regard to the test in Organic Analysis, he had discussed the matter with Prof. Christophus and they both agreed that instead of the test I should submit a thesis on 'Chelated Compounds' at a later date. On successful completion of these two requirements I should be eligible for the degree. I was very grateful and worked hard not to disappoint Prof. West.

Six weeks later Prof. West told me that I had completed satisfactorily the course in Physical Chemistry and I should now concentrate on the Thesis which should be submitted before the end of the academic year.

A strange situation developed reminiscent of relations in pre-war Poland when pickets of Polish anti-Semitic students stood outside University lecture halls barring the entrance of Jewish students to lectures. Did history repeat itself, though circumstances were so much different?

TRANSPORT TO BRITAIN

The border with Palestine had already been closed and the activities of the Haganah - the Jewish defence organisation - were growing in intensity. I was still formally in the Army, and in view of the growing hostility to Jewish students, I no longer wished to stay in Beirut. I reported my position to the Polish Authorities, who were very sympathetic and who suggested that I should join a transport of Polish families due to sail shortly to Britain. I was glad to accept the offer, and since I was the only officer in this group of Polish people, I was appointed Transport Commander. I welcomed the opportunity to go to Britain and hoped that I would be able to start soon on my thesis.

JUREK IN LONDON

My friend Jurek was still laid up in Casamassima hospital when I left the ward to join my Battalion. We kept in touch by letters. Soon after the end of the war I was surprised to get a letter one morning from him from somewhere in Scotland without giving any reasons for his being there. In a subsequent letter he informed me that he had been taken there to have an artificial leg fitted to his stump. Then there was a break in our correspondence and after many months, probably six or seven, he informed me from an address in London that he was getting married and would soon move into a house in West Kensington. He sent me a photograph of his fiancee, an attractive wench, and was unusually open about his happiness. I was delighted but wished to know a little more how it all happened. I decided that I would visit him as soon as I could after arrival in Britain.

The journey was quite pleasant though the ship 'Devonshire' was crowded and a number of people had to sleep on the deck. Every morning I received a report and a News sheet addressed to the O.C. Polish contingent. My task was to keep the people in my charge informed about progress of the journey, any special events like organised physical exercises, entertainment etc., to see that order and tidiness were observed, and generally to be a go-between between the Polish passengers and the ship's authorities. This kept me quite busy since there was no one else who could speak English.

My 'contingent' was a very mixed lot; some wives of airmen who fought in the Battle of Britain, a sizeable proportion of soldiers who took part in the Italian Campaign, and a large group of families originally from the Eastern provinces of Poland, who, after the invasion of that part by the Red Army, were banished to remote places of the Soviet Union, including Siberia, where some worked in Kolkhoses, some in factories in very harsh conditions. There were some youngsters whose education had been interrupted and who had spent four or five years of their youth trying to ease the parents' burden of earning a living.

There was, obviously, a lot of speculation about the future. In general people were optimistic. They had exaggerated views about English 'fair play'. The notion that an Englishman holds the Bible in one hand and a gun in the other had often been expressed. Convinced of the invincibility of the English, they often repeated a maxim that the English may lose a battle but never a war. There was a general belief among the people that an Englishman takes a bath every day, is very neat and tidy. It was difficult to know where those ideas came from, however, there were a few who were somewhat less enthusiastic but still believed that in the circumstances, settling in Britain was a good decision. Churchill was, of course, everybody's hero.

There were one or two cynics from whom I heard the following story: an English woman somewhere in the Middle East, Iran or Iraq, was in labour and the birth was particularly difficult. The attending nurse, having exhausted all her ingenuity, suggested to call a doctor. The doctor came, examined the patient and advised to take the woman quickly to the hospital for a caesarean. In the meantime there was some small progress, the baby was slowly moving out causing a lot of pain to the mother. A neighbour who was told what was going on next door rushed in and said that he could help; he had, he said, a very effective remedy. He took a swab of cotton wool, dipped it in petrol and brought it close to the nose of the appearing baby's head. The baby came out immediately.

We arrived in Tilbury in a grey, end of March morning, and the sight of the docks looked just as I imagined, dark, dirty and uninviting. However, we were all in good spirits, excited and in expectation of interesting changes.

Army lorries were waiting for us. I was approached by a Polish officer who explained the next move. We were going to a camp somewhere in Cheshire where we would be billeted in vacated British Army huts. Since the Authorities were still following traditional regulations, officers were directed to separate huts, and other rank and families to other ones. However, we all met together in the canteen where we took our meals.

A day or two after arrival I decided to do two things: to start writing my thesis and to contact Jurek. I needed scientific material and references for my writing and I had been advised that the best source for that purpose was Imperial College. I wrote to the Chemistry Department of the College enquiring whether I could be allowed to use their facilities for writing my thesis. A week or so later I received a positive reply and an encouragement to go ahead.

Soon I was on my way to London. It was April and London, the mention of which had always conjured up in my mind a picture of a town enveloped in mist, turned out to be bright and sunny, full of traffic and busy people. I made my way to Jurek's address. Travelling by tube was, of course, a novelty to me and quite an experience. I did not want to appear a country yokel and was careful not to ask too many questions. All I wanted was to be directed to West Kensington where I hoped to find Jurek's address. I managed to find the house, which had been severely damaged by a bomb and only part of it was still habitable. A strong embrace and an introduction to Joan, his newly married wife, followed.

The first thing I noticed was Jurek's tall wooden crutches when he got up from his chair to greet me. His shoulders were raised as a result of pressure of the crutches on his armpits, his posture bent forward to keep balance. I had not realised how short the stump of the missing leg was and this was the reason, as Jurek told me later, why the artificial leg that he was fitted with in a Scottish military hospital turned out to be useless. I saw it. It was a contraption with a harness and several straps, heavy and cumbersome, and meant for less severe cases and for strong men.

The flat they lived in consisting of two bedrooms, sitting room and kitchen, was part of the war damaged house, which they bought very cheaply. The furniture came from a junk shop and one or two pieces badly needed re-upholstering and the frames - a coat of varnish. The walls had been washed and the large Regency windows let in a lot of light. The atmosphere was pleasant and even cheerful. Joan - pretty, warm and gently smiling - gave the impression of having everything under control and being much in love with her husband. After some hours of recalling our experiences in the war and events after the war, Jurek told me how he met Joan.

When he was fit to leave the hospital, which was three or four months after I left, he was put, together with other severely injured soldiers, on an air transport to a hospital in Scotland which specialised in artificial limbs for war casualty cases. There they fitted him with the artificial leg. Some weeks later he was discharged and put on a train to London. Joan happened to be in the same compartment. She had been a nurse in the Forces and had also just been demobbed. There was a lot to talk about.

Somewhere in the Midlands the train crashed into another one. Passengers were thrown from their seats and rammed into the opposite walls of their compartments. Carriages mounted on one another, people were thrust through doors and windows. There was general panic. Miraculously, the carriage where Jurek and Joan were, escaped devastation though passengers were thrown from their seats and shaken up. Joan rushed to help the injured and worked for hours helping ambulance staff. Her part in the rescue operation was later described in glowing terms in the press. She also looked after Jurek and they both went on to London. This was the beginning of their romance which in a relatively short time culminated in marriage.

I told them that I would be spending some time at the Imperial College writing my thesis, whereupon they suggested that I should stay with them. I gladly accepted their hospitality.

Their meagre income came from Jurek's invalid pension and from letting a room with full board to a friend of theirs, a lecturer in mathematics at the Polish University College, which was established soon after the end of war to enable Polish students to continue their education. I decided to be as little a burden to Joan as possible and reduce my stay to a minimum. Though I wished to see something of London I was determined first of all to concentrate on my work, and in fact, for the following three weeks I got to know only the bus route to College and the local fish and chip shops.

The vastness of the Imperial College library impressed me greatly and at first I had difficulties in finding my way, however, the librarian, a friendly soul, proved very helpful. Soon I accumulated enough information to start on my writing. Five to six hours a day of solid work allowed me to progress quickly and before the end of three weeks, I was able to send off the hand written work to the American University of Beirut.

I got to like the college atmosphere, the beautiful building, the impressive lecture halls, the extensive laboratories and the mixture of races among students.

I returned to the Army Camp and had a period of leisure, not exactly carefree leisure, for there was still some anxiety with regard to the acceptability of my thesis. Most of the people in the camp had no idea what the future held for them. Over nearly five years their initiative had been taken away from them, they were directed by their superiors and as a result the ability to think for themselves atrophied. I always feared that this might happen to me but luckily the two years at the university and contact with civilians prevented the spread of that state of inertia.

The academic year at the AUB ended in June and in the beginning of July my degree arrived.

I heaved a sigh of relief and decided to relax for a while. The summer was exceptionally warm and the rich greenness of the countryside delighted the eye. My early social contacts with English people were made at the local pub. There I met a family of farmers whose property was adjacent to our camp and whose cottage was in a village about a mile away. A friendly lot they were. At times all three generations, grandma, husband and wife and their two daughters were in the pub, sitting round the table with their drinks in front of them. They were eager to know who we were, where we came from, what our plans were etc.

I, in turn, found out a bit about country life. After several encounters at the pub, my friend, with whom I used to go to the pub, and I suggested to the two young ladies to meet us the following day for a walk. They accepted the invitation and from then on we met frequently. They were prim and proper and we, against our instinct, unavoidably conventional.

A visit to Chester was a memorable occasion. It stimulated curiosity and whetted the appetite for knowledge of English history. But the reading of history had to wait until much later; in the meantime I kept an eye on possible jobs for chemists. After some weeks of scanning the ads columns of papers I came to the conclusion that there was no chance of getting a job as a chemist, but there were some openings for chemical engineers. This was a relatively new discipline and with some progress in industry, particularly in the petrol refinery industry, there was a need for chemical engineers. One day I noticed an announcement in the Times or Manchester Guardian about a postgraduate study in chemical engineering for graduate ex-servicemen. I immediately applied and a fortnight later was asked to come for an interview.

The Panel was a formidable one, or so it appeared to me.

There were five gentlemen sitting at a long beautifully polished mahogany table, two at each side and one at the top, in a large, high ceilinged room whose walls were covered with portraits of gentlemen with serious expressions on their faces. The building was that of the Institution of Electrical Engineers.

Why the panel was held there I never discovered.

I was naturally nervous and tried to overcome my anxiety by articulating my replies to questions with exaggerated firmness. I had no difficulty with the technical questions, but did not know what to say when I was asked about my hobbies. I had none at the time but didn't want to admit it, since I realised how important it was to an Englishman to have a hobby. I paused for a moment and said 'cycling'. I used to, I said, but for some years had no opportunity. This seemed to have satisfied the Chairman, though from his expression I felt he would have liked me to say 'stamp collecting, photography, or bird watching'. Again a period of apprehensive waiting. About a month later came a letter of acceptance with a promise of a monthly grant of £20. The annual postgraduate course was to be held at the South-West Essex Technical College and would start at the beginning of September. I had now less than a fortnight to find accommodation and to prepare for 'school'.

For the next two years my abode was a box room in a terraced house in Highams Park owned by a woman whose husband had mysteriously disappeared and who supported herself by letting two out of her three bedrooms to students or casual workers. At the time the only available room was the box room. I rented it because the price was low. A bed, a little desk and one chair, all three pieces from a junk shop, were the furniture of my room. I admired the landlady. She was hard working, never complained and always friendly to her lodgers. She was very happy when she had enough money to buy a television set.

My first job was not in chemical engineering - there were still very few vacancies in industry - it was as an assistant to a physicist in an analytical test laboratory of Edison-Swan Electric Company at Ponders End. My wages were £6 a week. I stood on my own feet. I was happy.

EPILOGUE

It was in October 1989 when on a visit to Israel my wife, Esther, and I went to the Museum of the Jewish Diaspora (Beit Hatefutsot) in Tel-Aviv where we were told that the Museum houses a large computer in which information is stored about Jewish communities in countries that were invaded by the Germans in the war. The computer responds to names of towns and villages where there had been a sizeable Jewish presence before the war, as well as to surnames, and produces the stored information in computer print. I typed out 'Jedrzejow' and out came a sheet with information about Jews in that town that I hitherto had very little knowledge of. I quote only excerpts. 'Jewish settlement there (in Jedrzejow) was prohibited until 1862, when Jewish families from the surrounding townlets and villages arrived in Jedrzejow. With the impetus given to the town's economy by the opening of a railroad station in 1884, the Jewish population rapidly increased. It numbered approximately 2050 (45% of total population) in 1897.

'The majority engaged in small scale trading and traditional crafts, and some were occupied in grain and timber trade. Jews with capital established timber and flour mills and mechanical workshops. The community was organised during the 1880s.

'...During the first weeks of Polish rule after the end of World War I there was a wave of anti-Jewish riots in the vicinity of Jedrzejow. According to the census of 1921, there were approximately 4600 Jews living in Jedrzejow (about 40% of the total population).'

'...During the 1930s, with mounting anti-Semitism, the struggle of the Jews to retain their economic positions in Jedrzejow became increasingly severe. In 1936 five Jews were murdered in the village of Stawy, near Jedrzejow.'

'...The German army entered on Sept. 4, 1939. In the spring of 1940 a Ghetto was established. In January 1941 about 600 Jews from the vicinity were concentrated in Jedrzejow. During the summer of 1942 another 2000 were transferred to the town from other nearby towns, increasing the Jewish population to about 6000. The entire Jewish population was deported in an 'Action' (a German euphemism for ruthless mass expulsion (auth.)) on Sept. 16 1942, to Treblinka death camp and only 200 men remained in a camp established inside the Ghetto. In February 1943 all two hundred were deported or shot, and Jedrzejow was declared 'Judenrein'.

'A number of Jews had succeeded in escaping from the Ghetto before the 'Action' took place but only a few survived in hiding; most of them were murdered by Polish gangs.'

This is an historical outline of the rise and tragic end of an entire community.

The agony of life in the Ghetto was described to me by my cousin, Mendel Horowich, who miraculously survived and who, on liberation, managed to emigrate to what was then Palestine. He was fortunate to be sent, together with a few others, to a munitions factory in a concentration camp near Skarzhisko, then to Theresienstadt where he was set free after the liberation by the Red Army. What he told me at length I shall relate in a very condensed form.

Two roads in the poorest part of town were cordoned off and assigned for a ghetto. As a result of the compulsory transfer of Jews from other small towns to Jedrzejow, the population density in the ghetto nearly doubled, and generally, two to three families occupied one room.

The Germans appointed a Judenrat (Jewish Council) whose task was to organise life in the ghetto, but their main task was to see to it that the required number of people for work was provided. Their other function was the distribution of food and fuel rations, and generally, to liaise with the German authorities. Judenrat members had some privileges and some of the counsellors behaved like scoundrels.

One of them, Mr. Z and his wife, occupied a three bedroom house, regularly appropriated 50% of the amount of coal allocated for the whole ghetto population, which he then sold at exorbitant prices. Mr. S, a generally respected gentleman with a reputation of honesty and righteousness, on being appointed second chairman of the Council, underwent a complete change of character. He became devious, corrupt and ruthless. It was in his power to save the lives of a dozen or so people who had hidden in the forest for some months, but could no longer survive in the severe condition of winter and starvation and decided to slip into the ghetto, but he preferred the quiet and safe life and denounced them all to the Germans who promptly shot them.

When in power and in anticipation of possible change of fortune, Mr. S made an arrangement with a Pole living outside the town to prepare for him a hideout. For this he paid with a lot of money and other possessions.

When the ghetto was liquidated the Judenrat members were sent to Auschwitz, but Mr. S succeeded in escaping from the transport and immediately made his way to his prepared hideout. But he did not enjoy it for long: the 'host' murdered him.

Only one of the Judenrat members, Mr. K., survived Auschwitz, but after liberation he had to hide from Jews who wished to settle their account for his conduct when he was councillor.

I used initials to avoid embarrassment which full names of the councillors might cause to members of their families.

My own family: mother, three sisters, one brother, brother-in-law and two nieces were taken away together with the others from the ghetto to the Treblinka death camp. Another brother died in Auschwitz to which Jews from Vienna were transported after some two years in Theresienstadt concentration camp.

My destiny was different. Some of my fellow prisoners died of exhaustion and starvation, some of typhoid, and a great number in battle. I was one of those who were taken on a compulsory journey and who were swept away by the tide of war, tossed and tumbled but allowed providentially to survive. In the scale of war time tragic events, my experience would be near the bottom, a mere seismic tremor compared with a devastating earthquake that had destroyed the lives of millions.

MAPS

Transport to Forced labour camp: Map 1 and Map 2. Route shown thus xxxxxxxxx.

1. My birthplace and town I started my journey from.
2. Crossed the river San - the temporary border between German occupied Poland and the Soviet Union occupied Eastern part of Poland.
3. Arrested soon afterwards and put in Sambor prison.
4. Transported by prison Police guarded open lorries to Voroshilovgrad with several stops at various prisons en route. This took about 12 months.
5. Transported by guarded lorries to Starobielsk, where sentenced without trial to 3 years of corrective lager (forced labour camp). Beginning of a 3 week journey in locked cattle railway wagons to the Far North.
6. Approximate location of Chibiu - the forced labour camp.

Journey to freedom: Map 3. Route shown thus -----------

7. Kuybyshev, where the Polish Army in the Soviet Union was formed.
8. Krasnovodsk - a port on the Caspian Sea where, together with other Polish subjects, I left the Soviet Union by

ferry to Bandar Shah in Persia (Iran).

Please note the difference in scale of the three maps.

    Map 1:   1 inch to 67 miles
    Map 2:   1 inch to 79 miles
    Map 3:   1 inch to 360 miles

REFERENCES

1. Majdalany Fred, 'Cassino, Portrait of a Battle' Popular Book Club, London 1945

2. Wankowicz Melchior, 'Bitwa o Monte Cassino' (in Polish) Wydawnictwo Kultury i Prasy Drugiego Polskiego Korpusu, Rzym (Rome) 1945 - Mediolan (Milan)

MAP 1

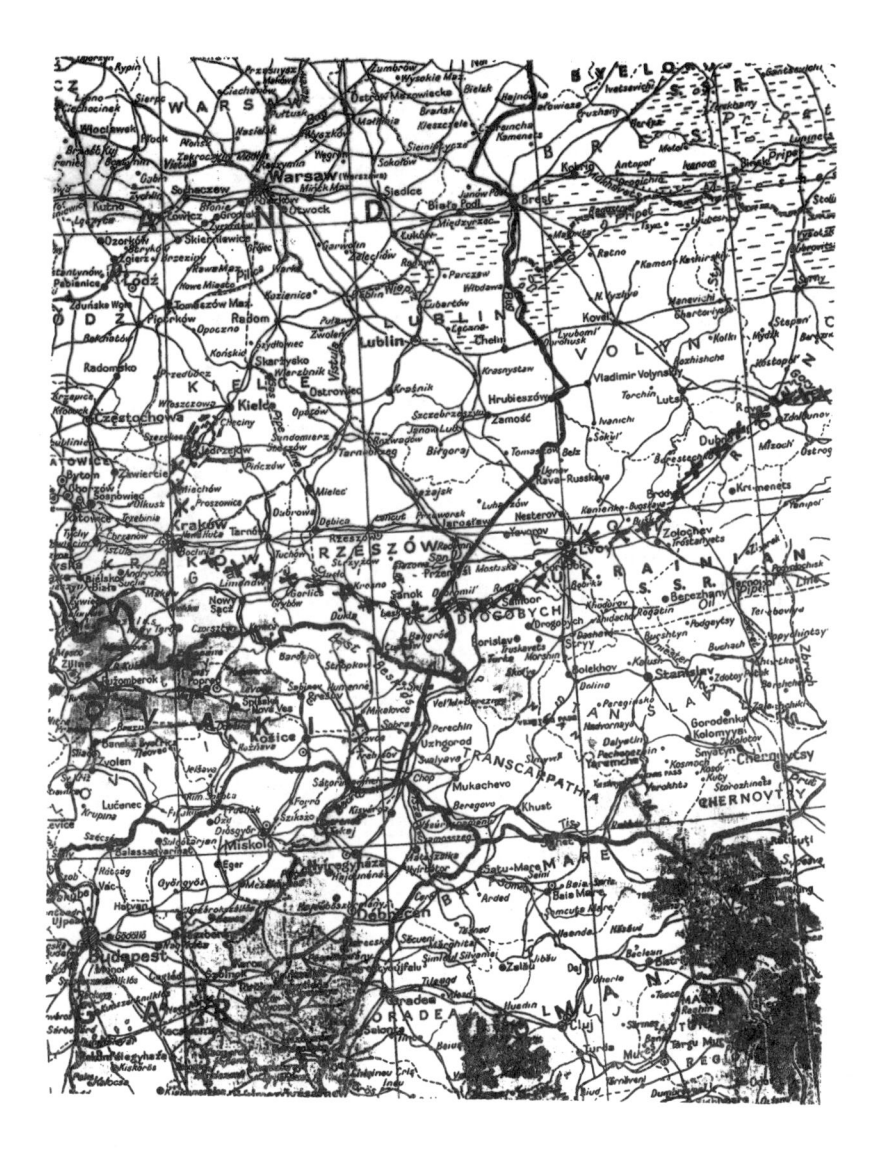

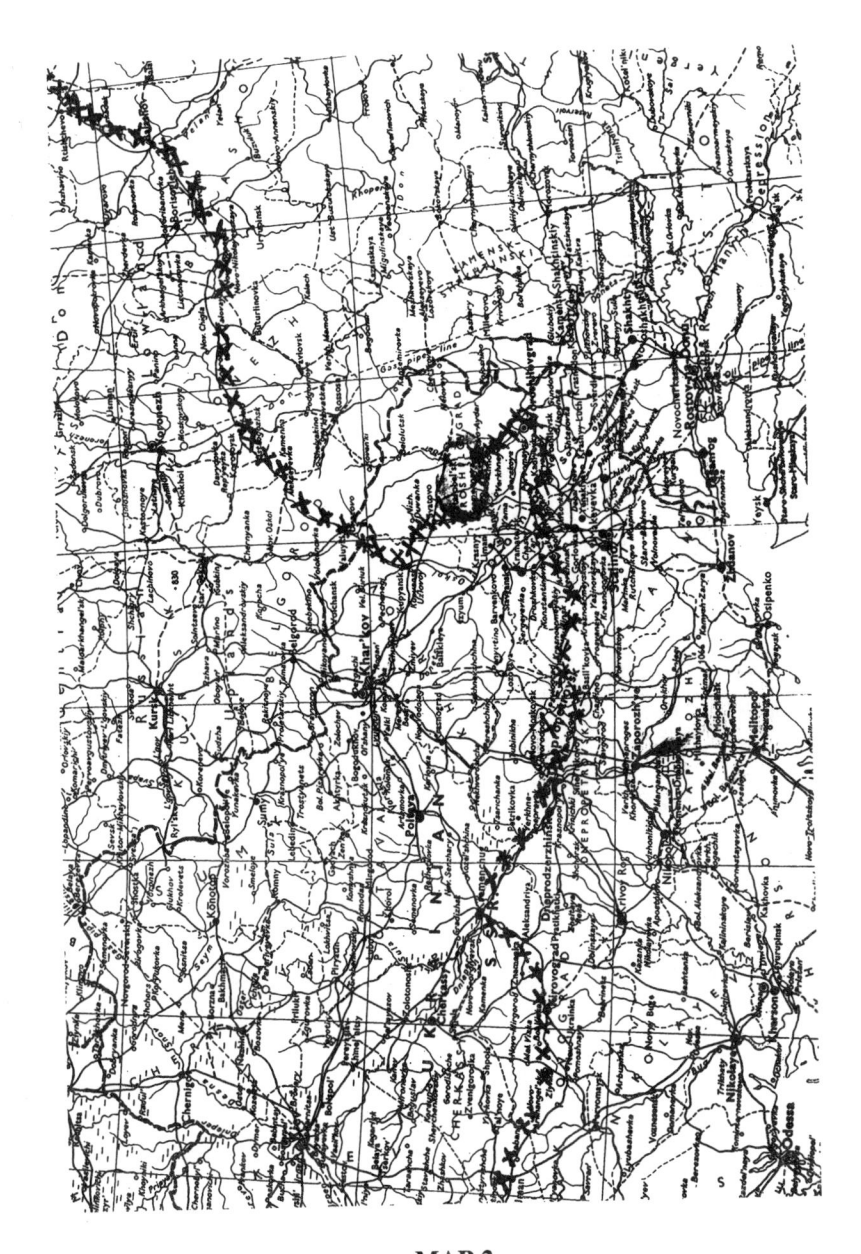

MAP 2

MAP 3

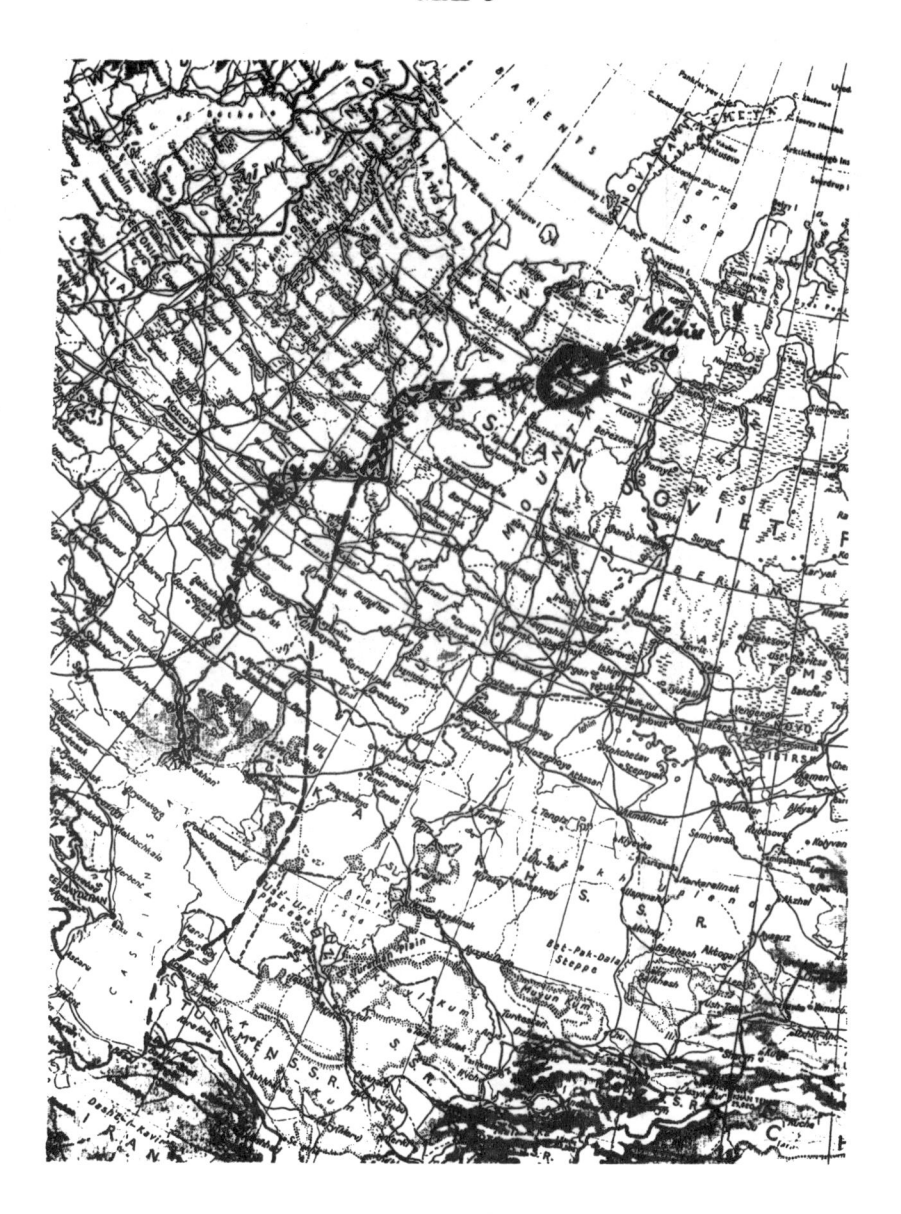